Visionary
Leadership
Skills

Creating a World to Which People Want to Belong

by

Robert B. Dilts

Dedication

This book is dedicated with much love and respect to
Gino Bonissone
who has taught me as much about life as he has about
leadership.

Meta Publications
P.O. Box 1910
Capitola, California 95010
(408) 464-0254
FAX (408) 464-0517

Library of Congress Card Number 96-075856
I.S.B.N. 0-916990-38-9

Contents

Acknowledgments

I would like to acknowledge:

Gino Bonissone and Ivanna Gasperini for their support and mentoring in my growth as a leader and as a person.

The late Todd Epstein who participated in bringing so many of my visions into reality.

The late David Gaster who introduced me to the notion of "visionary leadership", the magic of the word "mission" and the wisdom of Gilles Pajou.

Joe Yeager, who helped me to recognize the contributions NLP could make in the area of business and organization, and who formulated the "How to, Want to, Chance to" model.

Steve Arnold, who gave me the opportunity to explore the value of different media in teaching the skills of leadership.

Steve Pile who helped to widen my map of leadership.

Gregory Bateson and Bernard Bass for their wisdom and brilliance in understanding the context of leadership.

John Grinder and Richard Bandler for originating the methodology and approach upon which this work is based.

Ami Sattinger and Michele Roush who helped with the proof reading and editing of this book. Their commitment to excellence, and their deep desire for congruence has helped me to be a better writer.

The leaders involved in my study of leadership:

Gilles Pajou who provided both inspiration and examples of visionary leadership.

Andy Just who contributed editorial comments as well as serving as one of the models in my study.

Giovanni Testa who has continued to support the mission that this book represents for so many years.

Ginafranco Gambigliani who provided focus and support for the vision behind this work.

Preface

In 1988 a vision began to germinate within me about an extensive study of leadership skills based on the principles and distinctions of Neuro-Linguistic Programming. The study would include interviews and interactions with top managers in organizations throughout Europe and the United States.

At that time, the winds of change were blowing strongly across the world. Western Europe was gearing up for "1992", the EEC and the dream of a united Europe. Eastern Europe was poised to undergo profound ideological and economic changes. These dramatic developments were a reflection of an emerging new model of the world that is still effecting our whole planet. These developments have required not only a new concept of people, groups and culture, but have also called for a new set of skills for communicating and interacting with progressively larger systems of people. This book is both a result and a reflection of those times and their continuing influence.

It was during this period that I first met Gino Bonissone in Milan. Gino was working as a consultant in the areas of strategy formulation and organizational development. In each other, we found a remarkable combination of shared interests and complementary skills. Through time we were to become each other's mentors, students, colleagues and ultimately co-developers with respect to the applications of NLP to organizational leadership and change. The book *Skills for the Future* is one product of our continuing collaboration.

One of our first projects together was a study of effective leadership skills, focused at Fiat in Torino. This project proved to be a major contribution to my larger leadership study. The project was sponsored by Gianfranco Gambigliani and Giovanni Testa at Isvor Fiat; two men who possessed a brilliance, commitment and foresight that continues to impress me to this day. The companion volume to this book,

Modeling Effective Leadership Skills, describes both the process and results of that modeling project.

In May of 1989, my friend and fellow NLP trainer, the late David Gaster, introduced me to Gilles Pajou, the CEO of the French branch of the Swedish pharmaceutical company Pharmacia. Gilles was to become one of the central figures of my larger leadership study. His wisdom and words (which have been quoted throughout this book) embody many of the key characteristics of leadership. In fact, it is his definition of leadership as *"creating a world to which people want to belong"* (which serves as the title of this book) that, to me, most fully captures the goal and spirit of visionary leadership.

In June of 1989, I began a project with Steve Arnold of Lucasfilms involving a joint venture with Apple Computer to create a design example of an interactive multimedia program that would teach leadership, communication and systemic thinking skills to managers. The "communication matrix" was the result of the attempt to systematize some of the skills and intuitions of leaders for this project.

Another key event in the evolution of the vision that this book represents was the *Pathways to Leadership* conference, which I co-conducted with my late partner, Todd Epstein, in June of 1991. The Pathways to Leadership conference was dedicated to promoting the tools of NLP as a means to "create a world to which people want to belong". Much of the workshop and conference presentations focused on the applications of the different levels of change and leadership in organizations. In addition to a workshop, the program involved presentations from people who had been applying NLP in organizations and a symposium of people who were leaders from different fields.

While the substance of this book is rooted in the study of leadership in organizations and companies, the applications of the skills described within these pages are relevant to many situations. They can be an invaluable resource for people interested or involved in group and organizational work of any kind, including management, consulting, organizational development, training, teaching, even parenting.

Introduction

"Leadership is creating a world to which people want to belong" – Gilles Pajou

At some point in our lives we have probably all felt the desire to "change the world" or to "make the world a better place." This desire usually stems from a "vision" that our lives or our world could be enriched or improved in some way. Such visions of the future often provide guidance and direction for our lives and our work, furnishing the motivation and impetus for change. Visions that become shared by a number of people form the foundation of effective teamwork; and visions that become shared by multitudes constitute the basis for organization, culture and ultimately for the progress of civilization.

This book examines some of the essential skills and tools that are required to bring about change and "create a world to which people want to belong" – the skills and tools of "visionary leadership". These skills involve self exploration and discovery as much as they involve interacting with others. They relate to forming and clarifying one's own dreams and ideas, sharing those ideas with others, transforming dreams into actions and engaging the help of others to bring dreams and ideas into reality.

Many of the skills presented in this book have been modeled from and/or inspired by effective leaders and managers from around the world. They range from planning and problem solving, to communicating effectively and establishing rapport. Some of the topics to be covered include:

- Releasing natural leadership abilities through the identification of your vision and mission.

- Developing and maintaining states of personal excellence.

- Forming effective plans.

- Recognizing and addressing different thinking styles.

- Understanding and managing beliefs and belief systems.

- Enhancing personal effectiveness in communicating and in managing others.

- Exploring and enriching personal leadership styles.

- Giving useful feedback.

- Dealing with cultural presuppositions, organizational ecology and other systemic issues.

The most important aspect of developing leadership skills, however, involves engagement and commitment. The activities presented in this book are as important as the text. While some of the exercises in the book are best done in conjunction with others, most of the exercises are structured so that you can explore them on your own using a "fill in the blanks" approach. To get the most out of this book, however, it is essential to do the exercises either on your own or together with others. "Creating a world" involves as much action as it does vision.

Chapter 1

What is Leadership?

Overview of Chapter 1

- Defining Leadership
- The Problem Space of Leadership
- The Basic Skills of Leadership

Defining Leadership

One of the most important sets of skills required in a changing world are the skills of leadership. This has become increasingly evident as we have attempted to adapt to the escalating changes in our society and workplaces over the past century. As we try to take command of our own destiny and guide the destinies of our families, communities, organizations and our planet, the necessity of effective leadership ability has become increasingly obvious. Effective leadership is one of the keys to our future success and survival.

But what is leadership, and who has it? Can you develop leadership ability, or is it something you must be born with? Some say leadership has to be learned and earned. Others say leadership is a gift that cannot be taught.

Much of the literature on leadership focuses on "characteristics" of good leaders. These characteristics, however, are often too general to be of much practical value to someone trying to become a better leader. For instance, to say that good leaders are "gifted optimists" or are "honest" and "inspiring" provides little practical basis for specific skill development or improvement. These are typically judgments about our behavior made by others.

Frequently, descriptions of effective leadership emphasize what has been effective in a particular business, culture or environment. However, the actions, style or characteristics that make a leader "good" in one context may be ineffective or devastating in another.

Some studies of leadership focus on the outcomes of effective leadership; pointing out that good leaders "create vision," "mobilize commitment," "recognize needs," etc. However, simply knowing about these goals is not enough. The key to actually achieving them involves having the mental and behavioral skills required to put them into practice.

The purpose of this book is to define and explore some specific models, principles and skills that will allow you to be a more successful leader; i.e., the "how to's" of effective leadership.

In defining what effective "leadership" is, it is important to distinguish between (a) a "leader," (b) "leadership" and (c) "leading." The position of *"leader"* is a role in a particular system. A person in the formal role of a leader may or may not possess leadership skills and be capable of leading. *"Leadership"* is essentially related to a person's skills, abilities and degree of influence. A good deal of leadership can come from people who are not formal "leaders." *"Leading"* is the result of using one's role and leadership ability to influence others in some way.

In its broadest sense, leadership can be defined as *the ability to influence others toward the accomplishment of some goal.* That is, a leader leads a collaborator or group of collaborators towards some end. In businesses and organizations, 'leadership' is often contrasted with 'management'. Management is typically defined as *"getting things done through others."* In comparison, leadership is defined as, *"getting others to do things."* Thus, leadership is intimately tied up with motivating and influencing others.

In the emerging views of leadership, however, leaders do not have influence simply because they are 'bosses' or 'commanders'. Rather, leaders are people who are committed to "creating a world to which people *want* to belong." This commitment demands a special set of models and abilities in order to effectively and ecologically manifest the visions which guide those committed to change. It involves communicating, interacting and managing relationships within an organization, network or social system to move toward one's highest aspirations.

Nicholls (1988) has pointed out that a fair amount of confusion has arisen in leadership research because there are three fundamentally different perspectives of leadership. He defines these as *Meta, Macro* and *Micro.*

1. <u>Meta leadership</u> creates a 'movement' in a broad general direction (such as civil rights, home computers, or glasnost).   Meta leadership, *"links individuals, through the leader's **vision**, to the environment.   In doing so, it releases energy and creates enthusiastic followers."*

2. In <u>Macro leadership</u>, *"the leader's role in creating a successful organization is fulfilled in two ways; **path-finding** and **culture-building**...Path-finding can be summed up as finding the way to a successful future. Culture-building can be viewed as drawing people into purposeful organization – one which is capable of travel-ing along the path that is found or of fully exploiting current opportunities...Macro leadership activity can in-fluence individuals by linking them to the entity – be it the whole organization or just a division, department or group. The leader influences the individual by supplying the subordinates with answers to such questions as: What is this organization all about? Where do I fit in? How am I valued and judged? What is expected of me? Why should I commit myself? In the process, the leader creates committed members of the organization."*

3. In contrast to both of these, <u>Micro leadership</u> *"focuses on the choice of leadership **style** to create an efficient working atmosphere and obtain willing cooperation in getting the job done by adjusting one's style on the twin dimensions of task and relationship behavior. Choice of leadership style depends on the particular subordinates and the job/task being done; it is, thus, situational and contingent...the leader directs people in organizations in the accomplishment of a specific job or task. If the leadership style is correctly attuned, people perform willingly in an efficient working atmosphere."*

"Creating a world to which people want to belong" involves a mixture of all three different types of leadership ability to some degree.

The 'Problem Space' of Leadership

Before identifying some of the specific principles and skills that accompany micro, macro and meta leadership, let's look at some of the issues or 'problem space' those skills must address. The elements which make up a typical leadership situation involve (a) a leader leading (b) others toward (c) a goal within (d) a system. Thus, the general 'problem space' and skills of leadership (as perceived from the leader's perspective) involve managing the relationship between:

1. Oneself as a leader.

2. The desired goal or outcome of the project or situation.

3. The collaborators and others who influence and are influenced by oneself and the desired outcomes.

4. The system in which one is operating with others in order to reach the desired outcome.

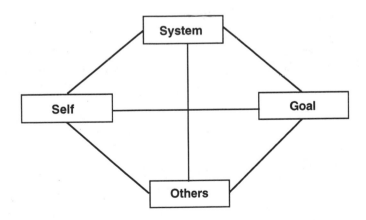

The General 'Problem Space' of Leadership

As Nicholls pointed out, however, the types of issues relating to this general 'problem space' of leadership will vary depending on whether one is engaged in meta, macro or micro leadership.

On a 'meta' level, for instance, leadership involves considering (a) one's mission with respect to (b) the larger global or overall system one is serving and (c) the community within which one is operating in relation to (d) the guiding vision that directs that system and community.

For example, Mohandas Gandhi expressed his spiritual mission to manifest what he called the 'soul force' in relation to the British and Indian communities within the tumultuous and war-torn world of the first half of the 20th century. He embodied his mission through his campaign for non-violent resistance in the service of the vision of a free and united India.

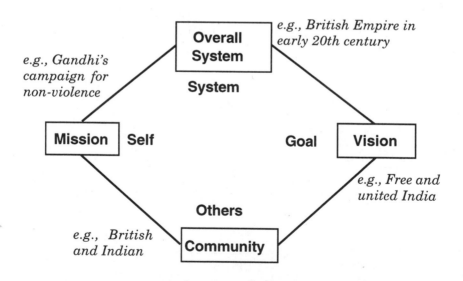

Problem Space of 'Meta' Leadership

On a 'macro' level, leadership involves considering (a) one's role within (b) an organizational structure and with respect to (c) the professional culture in which one is participating in order to define and pursue (d) the necessary path of objectives.

In the late 1980's, for instance, John Scully, acting within his role as president and CEO of Apple Computer, worked to create innovations in his company's organizational structure in order to develop and support the emerging 'high tech' culture of the company. This allowed the company to pursue a path leading to the stable incremental growth of the Macintosh computer in the personal computer marketplace.

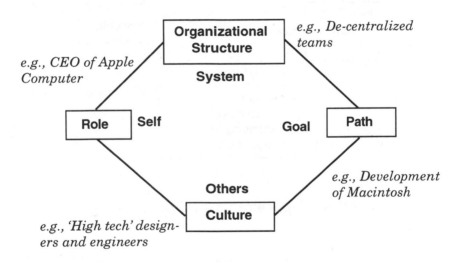

Problem Space of 'Macro' Leadership

On a 'micro' level, leadership involves considering (a) one's individual state and capabilities with respect to (b) the perceptual filters and motivations of one's collaborators in order to define and achieve (c) specific objectives in (d) a particular environmental context.

As an example, in order to stimulate new ideas and innovations for an animated film during a brainstorming session, Walt Disney had to use his own skills for creativity and communication. His success depended upon his ability to cycle between states of enthusiasm and focus while interacting with different animators, musicians, storywriters, producers, etc., in the storyboarding room at his studio.

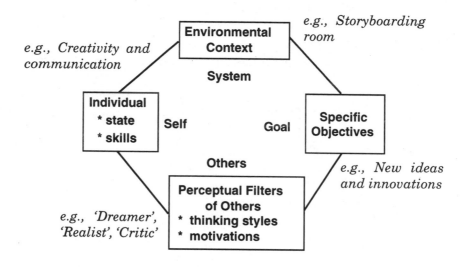

Problem Space of 'Micro' Leadership

The 'micro', 'macro' and 'meta' spaces of leadership must be defined, coordinated and aligned in order to produce effective and well-formed organizational actions.

For instance, it is important to consider one's *self* in relation to:

a) One's mission with respect to the larger system surrounding the organization.

b) One's role and responsibilities within the organization.

c) One's own personal history, values and capabilities as an individual.

Gandhi, for example, assumed different roles in his campaign for non-violence – including lawyer, author, editor and congressional representative – based on the evolution of his own skills, values and convictions.

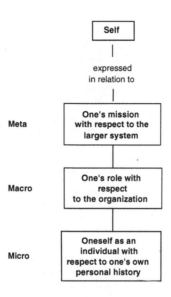

Leadership Issues Related to One's Self

Similarly, *goals* should be defined in relation to:

a) The longer term vision which guides a project or community.

b) The overall path of objectives necessary to move toward the vision.

c) The specific objectives which make up the steps along the path.

As an example, Disney's vision of a 'fantasy factory' had to be manifested through a path of developments marked by the completion of many specific projects and tasks. To prepare to make the animated masterpiece *Fantasia*, for instance, Disney's animators made many short films as practice and to provide financial support for the larger vision.

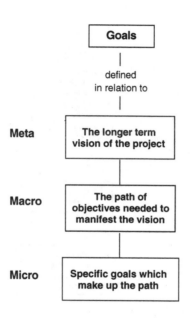

Leadership Issues Related to Goals

Collaborators and *others* may be understood with respect to:

a) The larger community of which they are members.

b) The professional or organizational culture to which they belong.

c) The particular perceptual filters and thinking styles they employ.

John Scully's challenges at Apple Computer not only had to do with his move from the East Coast to the San Francisco Bay Area community in California. He also had to make adjustments for the differences in professional cultures between Pepsi Cola and the high technology computer industry. He had to shift from a company culture primarily organized around marketing soft drinks and snack food, to one centered around the development of new computer hardware and software. In addition, he had to learn to deal with the differences in thinking styles and values between East Coast marketing managers and West Coast technology engineers.

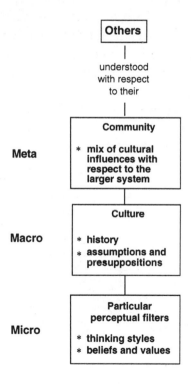

Leadership Issues Related to 'Others'

Finally, the leader needs to view the *system* in terms of:

a) The larger space of people and events which surround and influence the organization as well as its goals and needs.

b) The organizational structure which determines the general purpose and constraints for tasks and projects.

c) The specific situation that establishes the physical and relational conditions within which tasks and operations are to be implemented.

My own work, for example, involves doing training programs in many different parts of the world. To be effective, I not only need to take into account the different rooms and environments in which I am leading a particular seminar, I must also often make adjustments in order to meet the needs of different organizational structures. Beyond that, I need to consider the influence of different events and cultures occurring within the various parts of the world in which I am teaching.

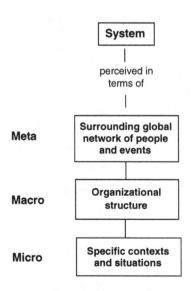

Leadership Issues Related to The System

In summary, effective leadership involves:

1) Considering the health and ecology of the larger systems of which the leader is a member.

2) Managing the balance of relationships and tasks in the achievement of organizational outcomes within a larger system.

3) Managing tasks and projects, through effective planning and the adjustment of leadership style.

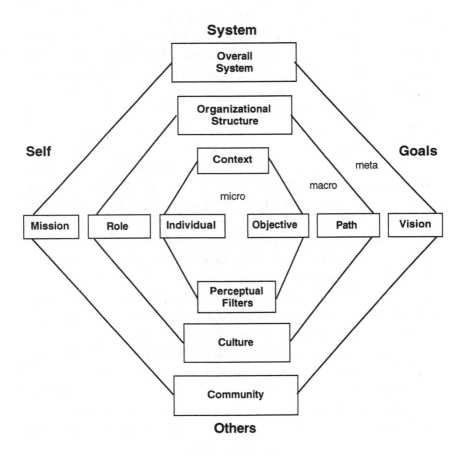

Space of Issues Related to Leadership

The Basic Skills of Leadership

The skills of leadership need to address each of the key elements which make up the 'problem space' of leadership: (a) oneself, (b) one's relationship with one's collaborators, (c) the system in which one is acting and (d) the goals to be achieved by oneself and one's collaborators in that system. This book covers a variety of skills addressing these various elements of leadership: self skills, relational skills, strategic thinking skills and systemic thinking skills.

Self skills have to do with how the leader conducts himself or herself in a particular situation. Self skills allow the leader to choose or engineer the most appropriate state, attitude, focus, etc., with which to enter a situation. In a way, self skills are the processes by which the leader leads himself or herself.

Relational skills have to do with the ability to understand, motivate and communicate with other people. They result in the ability to enter another person's model of the world or perceptual space, establish rapport and guide that person to recognize problems and objectives. Since leaders must reach their visions and accomplish their missions through their influence upon others, relational skills are one of the most essential aspects of leadership.

Strategic thinking skills are necessary in order to define and achieve specific goals and objectives. Strategic thinking involves the ability to identify a relevant desired state, assess the starting state, and then establish and navigate the appropriate path of transition states required to reach the desired state. A key element of effective strategic thinking is determining which operators and operations will most efficiently and effectively influence and move the present state in the direction of the desired state.

Systemic thinking skills are used by the leader to identify and comprehend the problem space in which the leader, his or her collaborators and the organization is operating. Systemic thinking is at the root of effective problem solving and the ability to create functional teams. The ability to think systemically in a practical and concrete way is probably the most definitive sign of maturity in a leader.

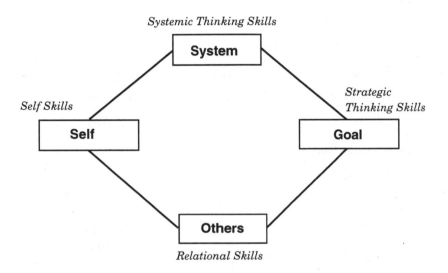

Basic Leadership Skills

My own professional mission involves work as a seminar leader, consultant, author, software developer and as director or co-director of several small companies and training organizations. This work involves operating with others one-on-one, in teams and with very large groups at times. Thus, I have had many opportunities to personally experience the various aspects of the 'problem space' of leadership defined in this chapter. My work has also provided me with the opportunity to practice and value all of these different types of skills, and experience their relevance to effective leadership. I think that they are all important aspects of 'creating a world to which people want to belong.'

Masteries of Leadership

The internalization of these skills will help you to master all of the key aspects of leadership. The following is a list of some of the 'masteries' of leadership we will be exploring in this book:

Mastery of Self (States)
> Aligning Vision and Action
> Congruence of Messenger and Message
> Awareness of Mental Maps and Assumptions

Mastery of Problem Space (System)
> Thoroughly Examining the System
> Finding the Relevant Elements and Issues
> Chunking Paths to Manageable Steps

Mastery of Communication (Messages)
> Developing Verbal and Non-Verbal Skills
> Using Different Representational Channels
> Interpreting and Managing Meta Messages

Mastery of Relationship (Rapport)
> Taking Multiple Perspectives
> Understanding Different Thinking Styles
> Recognizing Positive Intention

Chapter 2

Vision Into Action

Overview of Chapter 2

- Levels of Change and Leadership
- Moving From Vision to Action
- Effective Leadership and Internal States
- Creating an Aligned State
- Level Alignment Process
- Transcript: Demonstration of the Level Alignment Process
- Co-Alignment of Levels
- Level Alignment Worksheet

Levels of Change and Leadership

"Creating a world to which people want to belong" involves different levels of change and influence. In fact, the different types of leadership – 'meta', 'macro' and 'micro' – and the 'problem spaces' they involve, can be related to the 'level' of change that an individual or organization is attempting to influence.

For instance, there's the *where* and the *when* of the 'problem space' of change. This relates to particular environments and environmental influences, such as physical space and time constraints, that might influence a problem or goal.

Then there's the *what* related to a particular context. This refers to the behavioral activities or results to occur within the environment – i.e., *what* is supposed to happen in a particular *where* and by *when*.

Of course, people's actions are not only determined by their external environment. Different individuals may exhibit a wide variety of behavioral reactions to similar environmental cues and constraints. What accounts for these behavioral differences? Variations in people's mental maps and perceptions. Outcomes and responses on a behavioral level are directed by cognitive processes; that is, by *how* people are thinking about something or mentally representing it. The *'how'* level of change relates to people's inner maps and cognitive capabilities.

The process of change is also greatly influenced by people's beliefs and values. These relate to the *why* of a particular problem or outcome. Why, for instance, should a person consider changing his or her thoughts or actions? A person's degree of motivation will determine how much of his or her own inner resources he or she is willing to mobilize. Motivation is what stimulates and activates *how* people think and *what* they will do in a particular situation.

There is also the *who* involved in the process of change. Which roles and functions are involved in the problem or outcome? *Who* is supposed to be involved? What beliefs, values, capabilities and behaviors are associated with the various roles?

Finally, there's the *who and what else,* involving the larger system or vision surrounding specific roles, beliefs, capabilities, actions, etc. This level relates to what could be considered the vision and 'spirit' of an organization or system.

As these distinctions indicate, our brain structure, language, and social systems form natural hierarchies or levels of processes. The function of each level is to synthesize, organize and direct the interactions on the level below it. Changing something on an upper level would necessarily 'radiate' downward, precipitating change on the lower levels. Changing something on a lower level could, but would not necessarily, affect the upper levels.

The levels I have identified here were inspired by the work of anthropologist Gregory Bateson (1972), who identified several fundamental levels of learning and change. Each level is more abstract than the level below it, but each has a greater degree of impact on the individual or system. These levels roughly correspond to:

'Spiritual'	Vision & Purpose
A. *Who I Am* – Identity:	Role & Mission
B. *My Belief System* – Values, Meta Programs:	Motivation & Permission
C. *My Capabilities* – States, Strategies:	Perception & Direction
D. *What I Do* – Specific Behaviors:	Actions & Reactions
E. *My Environment* – External Context:	Constraints & Opportunities

The environmental level involves the specific external conditions in which our behavior takes place. Behaviors without any inner map, plan or strategy to guide them, however, are like knee jerk reactions, habits or rituals. At the level of capability, we are able to select, alter and adapt a class of behaviors to a wider set of external situations. At the level of beliefs and values we may encourage, inhibit or generalize a particular strategy, plan or way of thinking. Identity, of course, consolidates whole systems of beliefs and values into a sense of self. The 'spiritual' level relates to our perceptions and maps of those parts of our larger system which are beyond ourselves. While each level becomes more abstracted from the specifics of behavior and experience, it actually has more and more widespread effect on our behavior and experience.

- **Environment** determines the external opportunities or constraints to which a person has to react. It involves the *where* and *when* of leadership — influencing the external context. The 'environmental' level of leadership primarily relates to people's *reactions*. It consists of things such as the type of room, food, noise level, etc. that surrounds a situation. Certainly these external stimuli will effect the responses and the state of a leader and his or her collaborators. One key aspect of leadership skill has to do with attention to the physical environment.

- **Behaviors** are the specific actions or reactions made by a person within the environment. It involves the *what* of leadership — influencing people's *actions*. The 'behavioral' level of leadership has to do with the specific behavioral activities that the leader and his or her collaborators must engage in. The specific behaviors that people actively participate in, such as tasks and interpersonal interactions, often serve as the primary evidence for organizational goals. Much of the focus of leadership has traditionally been on the level of behavior.

- **Capabilities** guide and give direction to behavioral actions through a mental map, plan or strategy. The level of 'capabilities' relates to the *how* of leadership — influencing people's minds. 'Capabilities' have to do with the mental strategies and maps collaborators develop to guide their specific behaviors. Simply prescribing behaviors does not insure that tasks will be accomplished and goals reached. The function of the level of capabilities is to provide the *perception* and *direction* necessary to achieve particular objectives.

- **Beliefs and Values** provide the reinforcement that supports or inhibits capabilities and behaviors. The level of 'beliefs and values' involves the *why* of leadership — influencing people's hearts.   In addition to developing behavioral skills and capabilities, an effective leader must also address the presuppositions, beliefs and values of his or her collaborators. The degree to which some task fits (or does not fit) into the personal or cultural value systems of one's collaborators will determine the degree to which they accept or resist that task. Beliefs and values influence the amount of *motivation* and *permission* collaborators experience with respect to their roles and tasks.

- **Identity** involves a person's role, mission and/or sense of self. It relates to the *who* of leadership. The 'identity' level has to do with the sense of self experienced by a group or group members. Identity is somewhat difficult to define precisely. It is more abstract than beliefs and has to do with the deepest levels of incorporation of information, responsibility for what one has learned, and the commitment to put it into action. Identity has primarily to do with *mission*.

- **'Spiritual'** change relates to the larger system of which one is a part and the influence of that system on the group or organization. It involves the *who else and what else* of leadership — influencing the larger system. 'Spiritual' factors come from our perception of being a part of larger and larger systems surrounding us. It determines the overall *vision* or purpose behind the actions of an individual or organization.

Clearly, each level of change involves progressively more of the system, or a larger 'problem space'. Each level involves different types of processes and interactions that incorporate and operate on information from the level below it. In this way they form a network of "nested" processes as shown in the following diagram.

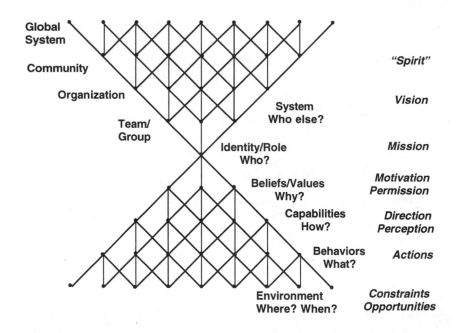

Levels of Leadership

Effective leadership clearly involves addressing issues at all of these levels – whether it be in regards to self, others, system or goals.

Micro leadership primarily addresses issues at the levels of environment, behavior and capability: i.e., where, when, what and how.

Macro leadership focuses on issues at the levels of beliefs, values and role identity: i.e., the why and who behind the where, when, what and how.

Meta leadership emphasizes the levels of 'spirit' and identity: i.e., the who and what else which form the vision and purpose behind all of the other levels of leadership.

Moving From Vision to Action

The typical path of change in intelligent organizations involves moving from the level of vision to that of action. Meta, macro and micro leadership ability is required to stimulate and manage the various processes that make up the pathway between vision and action.

Meta leadership provides inspiration and motivation by forming the vision into a mission and creating community within a system. Macro leadership creates the strategy for manifesting the vision and mission by defining the values, culture and path for reaching the desired state. Micro leadership supplies the structure to make the culture and path concrete through specific tasks and relationships.

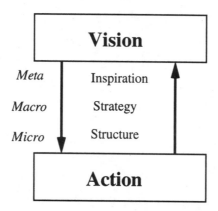

Different Types of Processes and Leadership Ability are Involved in the Movement From Vision to Action

The following exercise provides a way to combine both systemic thinking and strategic thinking in order to create a vision and then define a path leading from that vision to the actions that will concretely embody it.

Exercise: Vision Into Action

What I see way off is too nebulous to describe. But it looks big and glittering. — **Walt Disney** (1941)

Part I. Creating a Vision

1. Put yourself in a relaxed and open state in which you can feel fully yourself.

2. With your eyes closed, create a space for 'Vision' in your mind's eye. Imagine a vast inner 'landscape'. Notice where the horizon of your inner landscape is.

   Also notice the 'point of convergence' or 'vanishing point' related to your focus with respect to the inner landscape. Note how far from the tip of your nose this vanishing point appears to be. Is it one meter? 10 meters? A kilometer?

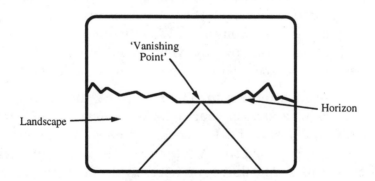

Extend the point of convergence until it is farther away. If you need to, you can lower your horizon. Find a vanishing point that represents the rest of your life. Then, extend your focus far beyond that point. As you do, lengthen your spine and lift your head slightly.

Imagine a sunrise breaking over the horizon. Feel what it is like to experience the dawning of a new day. Let the feeling of hope and belief in the future emerge.

From this state ask yourself the question, "What is my vision?" Let the images and words of your answer form out of your feeling and the light coming from the sunrise.

3. Bring your attention and focus back to the point representing the rest of your life, maintaining the awareness of the sunrise and the feeling associated with your vision. Consider what needs to be done in that time frame in order to move towards the vision. Ask yourself the questions, "What is my mission with respect to that vision?" "What is my role and identity with respect to the larger system associated with that vision?" "What is a symbol or metaphor for that role and mission?"

4. Focus your attention on your body and the feelings and emotions associated with your sense of vision and mission – especially those that draw you toward them. Feel the sense of motivation, inspiration and excitement that you have about the future. Imagine that you could give your heart a 'voice' so that these feelings could be put into words. Ask yourself, "What values are expressed and represented by my vision and mission?" "What beliefs are associated with my vision and mission?"

5. Shift your attention to your spine and chest. Lengthen your spine and open your chest so you can breathe more fully and freely. Feel a sense of physical energy and strength in your body. Ask yourself the question, "What capabilities do I have, or need to develop, in order to support my beliefs and values and reach my mission with respect to my vision?"

6. Bring your focal point near to you, finding what feels like a close but comfortable distance. Allow your awareness to go into your belly and the muscles and bones of your body. Ask yourself the question, "What is my next step toward achieving my mission?" "What internal state will most help me to reach that step?" Form a plan for taking that next step.

7. Imagine that you are physically moving forward and associating into that point in the future and the context it represents. Ask yourself the question, "When and where will I complete this next step?"

Part II. Defining Your Path

Complete the answers in the spaces beneath each of the following questions in order to define the connecting links between the various levels of processes that you have been exploring. These links will form the path between your vision and the actions necessary to manifest that vision.

1. "What is your *vision* with respect to the *larger system* or community in which you are operating?"

My/Our vision is to

_____

2. "What is your *identity* or role with respect to your vision and the system or community to which you belong?"

"*Who* are you or do you want to be in relation to the manifestation of your vision?" (Try using a metaphor or symbol to answer this question.)

In relation to that vision, I am/we are

_____

"What is your mission with respect to that system and vision?"

My/Our mission is to

_____

3. "What *beliefs* and *values* are expressed by or encompassed by your vision and mission?"

"What values are embodied by your role identity and larger vision?"

I am/We are committed to this vision and mission because I/we value

_____

"*Why* do you have this particular vision and mission? What beliefs provide the motivation for your thoughts and activity?"

I/We believe

_____

4. "What *capabilities* are needed to manifest your vision and achieve your mission, given the beliefs and values that you have expressed?"

"*How* will you accomplish your mission? What capabilities and cognitive processes are needed or presupposed in order to accomplish your vision within the guidelines of your beliefs and values?"

To accomplish my/our vision and mission I/we will use my/our capabilities to

_____

5. "What is the specific *behavior* associated with manifesting your vision and achieving your mission that will both use your capabilities and fit with your beliefs and values?

"What is your plan for achieving your vision and mission? *What,* specifically, will you do to accomplish your mission? What specific actions are associated with your vision?"

My/Our plan is to

_____

_____

6. "What is the *environment* in which you will manifest your vision and reach your desired state?"

"*When* and *where* do you want to enact the behaviors and actions associated with your vision and mission? What will be the external context surrounding the desired goal and activities?"

This plan will be implemented in the context of

_____

An Example of a Path From Vision to Action

I have used this process many times in order to create and organize paths for manifesting my own visions. The following, for instance, is an example of how I answered these questions while preparing for this work on leadership.

My vision is to promote the worldwide diffusion of more effective and ecological tools and skills for leadership.
In relation to that vision, I am like a spring and a reservoir for special knowledge and experiences.
My mission is to develop, integrate and present practical skills that will help people of all types to be better leaders.

I am committed to this vision and mission because I value growth, the achievement of our highest expression and the fundamental integrity of life.

I believe in the value of the future and that people can truly grow and change their lives through the acquisition of new skills. I also believe that the skills of leadership are essential in order to fulfill our destiny on this planet.

To accomplish my vision and mission I will use my capabilities to identify, structure, and articulate the key principles and skills of leadership that I have modeled from effective leaders throughout the world.

My plan is to create leadership seminars, manuals, books and other tools that can be disseminated to individuals, organizations and social systems worldwide.

This plan will be implemented in the context of a global network of people who are committed to promoting the progress of all humanity.

Creating an Image of Your Vision

When you have finished defining your path from vision to action, create a picture of your overall vision. This will help you to consolidate your sense of your vision and mission, remember it, and communicate that vision to others. Below is an example of my picture for my own vision.

Representation of My Vision for My Leadership Work

Effective Leadership and Internal States

"Leadership is more a state than an activity."
– Gilles Pajou

Manifesting our visions is only partially a result of our plans and strategies. A good deal of what happens during the process of leadership is unconscious. Many key aspects related to implementing a path to a vision and managing leadership situations often occur outside of conscious awareness. They come in the form of insight or inspiration. In addition to instruments and tools that allow us to bring our visions and the path for their realization into awareness, it is also useful to have some ways of encouraging and actually directing or utilizing unconscious processes as well. This is most effectively done through the management of our internal states.

Leadership ability is a function of a person's state as well as his or her conscious mental processes. In this sense, effective leadership performance is similar to other types of performance. Athletes getting ready to perform, prepare their internal state as much as they physically prepare themselves. Similarly, effective leadership is influenced by a person's internal state.

For instance, one of the questions I asked in my study of leadership was, "How do you deal with challenging situations involving uncertainty, incongruity and/or complexity?" The most common reaction to this question went something like:

"Even though I prepare myself well before I go into a challenging situation, when I actually am in that

situation I do not really think about what I am going to do or say or how I should react or respond. There are too many things that could come up that I haven't thought of. At that time there is only one thing on my mind: 'What state do I want to be in?' Because if I am in the right state the inspiration will come."

Thus, in addition to the mental strategies and skills related to leadership, there are also the purely physiological aspects that help to access and integrate unconscious processes. As an example, the founder of a large shipping company claimed that he used physical activities to help him solve problems. For certain problems, he would have to go out and play golf to get into the frame of mind required to deal with the issues. For other problems, he would go out and ride his bicycle in order to think about it effectively. He was so specific about which type of physiology to use that he would say, "You can't golf on that problem. That's one that you have to ride your bicycle on."

The point is that our internal physiological state stimulates and organizes other neurological activities. Riding a bicycle is an example of one way to activate and maintain a particular state.

In many ways the most fundamental instrument of leadership is your own body and nervous system. You could go so far as to say that the manifestation of all leadership ability comes through your body or physiology in some way. It comes into the world through your words, voice tone, facial expression, body posture, the movement of your hands, etc. And your ability to use these most fundamental instruments of leadership is greatly dependent on your internal state.

In fact, sometimes leadership ability can be too state-dependent. A good analogy is provided by the American movie "Butch Cassidy and the Sundance Kid." The Sundance Kid was a gunfighter who was a great shot, but he could only shoot if he was moving. If he tried to stand still, he couldn't hit anything, he had to be jumping, falling or twisting in order to aim. This is an advantage but can also be a limitation. Similarly, some people can only perform effectively when they're under stress.

There is a saying that, "When the going gets tough, the tough get going." The implication is that a difficult situation forces strong people to draw more fully on their inner resources. The problem arises for these kinds of people when there is no difficult situation. They have to create one in order to get going.

Thus, one of the most important 'self skills' of leadership is the ability to manage one's internal state. This involves the capacity to select and maintain the types of internal states that will promote and sustain effective leadership performance.

Creating an Aligned State

One of the most important aspects of effective leadership is the congruence between the 'message' and the 'messenger'. On a personal level, an effective leader is one whose own actions are aligned with his or her capabilities, beliefs, values and sense of identity or mission. A person's sense of role and identity is a dynamic process related to several different factors:

1) One's sense of mission or purpose (which evolves with one's cycle of development in life).

2) One's view or vision of the larger system of which one is a part (a 'spiritual' perspective).

3) One's role in relation to the organizational and family systems of which one is a member.

The concept of different 'levels' of leadership provides us with a powerful road map for bringing the various dimensions of ourselves into alignment in order to realize our visions. Each of these different levels is embodied through successively deeper and broader organizations of 'neural circuitry'. As one moves from the simple perception of the environment, for instance, to the activation of behavior within that environment, more commitment of one's mind and body must be mobilized.

Capabilities call into play longer term plans and maps, and require the involvement of even deeper levels of the nervous system. Beliefs and values are represented and manifested through the mobilization of neurology that calls into play structures as deep as the autonomic nervous system (such as the heart and 'guts'). Identity involves the total commitment of our nervous systems. 'Spiritual' experiences involve the resonance between our own mind and nervous system with the larger systems of which we are a part.

The following process provides a way to systematically access and connect experiences and neural processes associated with each of these different levels. By combining mental and physical processes with the different levels of leadership and change, a person can bring all these levels into alignment in the service of their vision and mission.

The process uses what is called 'spatial anchoring' to activate and integrate these different levels of experience. Many people have found this to be a very powerful experience and a tool to put themselves into an effective 'aligned' state for leadership.

Level Alignment Process

Start by physically laying out a space for each of the six levels of leadership.

Spiritual	Identity	Beliefs/Values	Capabilities	Behaviors	Environment

1. Start by standing in the "Environment" space and answering the question: "When and where do I want to be more aligned as a leader?"

2. Move to the "Behavior" space and answer the questions: "What do I need to do when I am in those times and places?" "How do I want to act?"

3. Stand in the "Capabilities" space and answer the questions: "How do I need to use my mind to carry out those behaviors?" "What capabilities do I have or need to have in order to carry out those actions in those times and places?"

4. Step into the "Beliefs/Values" space and answer the questions: "Why do I want to use those particular capabilities to accomplish those activities?" "What values are important to me when I am involved in those activities?" "What beliefs do I have or need to guide me in my heart when I am doing them?"

5. Move to the "Identity" space and answer the questions: "Who am I if I have those beliefs and values and use those capabilities to accomplish those behaviors in that environment?" "What is a metaphor or symbol for my identity and mission?"

6. Stand in the "Spiritual" space and answer the questions: "Who and what else am I serving?" "What is the vision beyond me that I am participating in?"

7. Maintaining the physiology and inner experience associated with the "Spiritual" space, step back into the "Identity" space. Combine and align your 'spiritual' level and 'identity' level experiences. Notice how your 'spiritual' level experience enhances or enriches your initial representation of your identity and mission.

8. Take the experience of both your vision and your identity and bring them into your "Belief" space. Again notice how this enhances or enriches your initial representation of your beliefs and values.

9. Bring your vision, identity, beliefs and values into the "Capabilities" space. Experience how they strengthen, change or enrich the capabilities you experience within yourself.

10. Bring your vision, identity, beliefs, values and capabilities into the "Behavior" space. Notice how even the most seemingly insignificant behaviors are reflections and manifestations of all of the higher levels within you.

11. Bring all levels of yourself into the "Environment" space and experience how it is transformed and enriched.

12. Memorize the feeling of this aligned state. Imagine yourself being in this state at key times and places in the future when you will most need it.

This process may be done by oneself or together with another person acting as a consultant or 'guide'. The following is a transcript showing how one person may guide another through the process of creating an aligned state.

Transcript: Demonstration of the Level Alignment Process

RBD: I would like to demonstrate the level alignment process with J. The first step is to physically lay out six spaces for each of the different levels; one for environment, behavior, capabilities, beliefs and values, identity and 'spiritual'. I generally like to place them one behind the other, so that you step back as you move from the 'environment' to the 'spiritual' locations; and step forward as you move from the 'spiritual' space to the 'environmental' space.

J: OK.

RBD: And what I'm going to ask you to do first, J., is to stand in the environment space and think about the environment in which you would like to be more personally aligned.

J: Well, I'm a manager, and I would like be more aligned in my job.

RBD: Can you describe some of the environments that you work in as a manager? The question being, "Where and when do you function as a manager?" Describe some specific times and places that you engage in your job.

J: Usually I'm in my office at our headquarters. I could also be in a meeting room, like this one, but a little bit smaller. There are a number of people that come and go. I primarily interact with about a dozen key people on a daily basis. Usually it is during the week, sometimes on the weekends.

RBD: O.K. Very good. (To audience) Notice how J. described these in a very matter of fact way – which is very appropriate for environmental level descriptions. Your environment is simply what you see and hear around you. People are often tempted to make judgments or interpretations about their environments as opposed to describe just what they see and hear. If someone said, "I work in a hostile environment," that would be a judgment about their environment. For this process, at this level, it is important to describe only what you sense externally, as J. did.

(To J.) Now, I'd like to have you step into the behavior space and describe the kinds of things that you do when you are effectively managing those people in those places and at those times. The question is, "What do you want to do more of in those 'wheres' and 'whens'?" "What are the actions and behaviors that you engage in, at those times and places when you are being an effective manager?"

J: I could be standing, sitting or walking around. Sometimes I'm talking, sometimes I'm presenting ideas or negotiating with people. Sometimes I'm trying to support people by asking questions and saying things to them and writing things down. So I'm listening, asking questions, trying to make sense out of what people are saying and doing, and then trying to give them guidance or keep them on track.

RBD: Good. (To audience) Again, notice how J. is simply describing a set of behaviors – not making interpretations. If he had said, "I behave well or poorly," these would be judgments about behaviors. For this exercise, at this level, 'behaviors' would be actions that a video camera would be able to record if it was in the environment. Video cameras don't judge or interpret, they just record.

(To J.) I'd like to stay with the behavior level a bit longer and try to define a few of the 'micro' behaviors that would go along with being more 'aligned'. Pay attention to your body for a moment and get a sense of how your posture would be if you were aligned while you were sitting, standing or walking in your office environment. How would you be holding your body?

J: (Stands more erect and symmetrical) I'd be balanced and centered. I guess my head would be back and slightly up.

RBD: What would you be doing with your hands? What kinds of gestures do you make when you are aligned?

J: (Moving his arms) I think I reach out to people more, and make more eye contact.

RBD: Do you notice anything different or special about your breathing when you are aligned?

J: It is slower and deeper.

RBD: What about your voice? How does your voice sound when you are aligned?

J: It's softer; a bit more resonant and inquisitive. It also seems clearer and more even.

RBD: That's nice. Now I'd like you to step back to the capabilities space. And the question here is, "How are you able to do those 'whats' in those 'wheres' and 'whens'?" In other words, "What is the know-how or the mental strategies and skills you need in order to listen, ask questions, and guide people in a way that's balanced, centered, clear and even?"

J: Well, I need to use my capability to structure things and to organize information. I need my professional knowledge to put that structure into words, action and behavior. I also need my capability to put myself into the shoes of others and see things from their perspective. And, I need my ability to go to an 'observer' position, seeing the relationship between myself and others. I also need to use my capability to make pictures of what I'm going to do.

RBD: O.K. (To audience) Notice how J.'s physiology changes as he steps into each new space. The amount of gestures and movements increases. He literally involves more of himself, and consequently his neurology, at each level. In the environment space he hardly moved at all. In the behavior space he began to gesture with his arms and move around a little. In the capability space, you could see his eyes moving and searching around more as he accessed his skills and abilities. Also, as he describes the different levels, there is a change in his tone of voice. He speaks a bit more slowly and deeply. The types of words he uses changes. They indicate more broad reaching personal processes.

(To J.) What mental abilities do you need in order to maintain the physical expression of your aligned state? What are the inner capabilities that allow you to be balanced and centered, reaching out to people, breathing more deeply and speaking more softly and clearly?

J: The ability to hold my personal goals clearly in mind and to see how they fit the situation. Also, the capability to maintain a feedback loop with myself, and between myself and others. I guess primarily it would be my ability to be aware of myself and what I want, and the quality of my relationship with my collaborators.

RBD: Great. Now, I'd like to have you step into the belief space. The question here is, "Why do you use those particular capabilities to act in those ways in those environments? Why do you choose to use your abilities to structure, to put things into words, to look at things from other perspectives, to picture what you are going to do, to be aware of yourself and others and to get feedback? What sort of beliefs and values lead you to use that know-how and to take those actions in those times and places?"

J: Well, I believe in respect; respect for other people. I also believe in having good relationships. I believe in support for other people and myself, in order to enrich what we can do together. I believe that it is important to have integrity, and that it's good to have a lot of skills in order to accomplish things.

RBD: So you value respect, relationships, support, skill and integrity. Those are important and powerful values. (To audience) The question we are exploring here is "What beliefs do you have about yourself, about people, and about doing what you do?" What beliefs guide you? Notice how J.'s voice became even deeper. It is almost as if you hear even more of him speaking. He is speaking from his heart.

(To J.) I'd like to have you now step back to the identity space and answer the question "Who am I that, in my heart, I would respect the lives of others, want good relationships, support people, value lots of skills and believe in integrity?" "Who am I that I would use my mind to create structure, to put things into words, to take multiple perspectives, visualize the future and maintain an awareness of myself and my goals?" "Who am I that I have developed the strengths to present ideas, to sit, stand, walk around, listen, ask questions and respond to people in those rooms during the week and sometimes on the weekends on that part of this planet where my office is located?" "Who am I as a manager?"

What kind of a manager are you? What kind of a person are you? What is your metaphor for yourself and your mission?

J: (Pause) Well, one metaphor would be that I am like a lighthouse. I am a lighthouse that shows people the way and helps them to get there.

RBD: So, you are like a lighthouse that gives support and direction to people. This is a metaphor or symbol for your sense of identity and mission.

I'd now like to ask you to take final a step beyond being a lighthouse, into a space that transcends yourself – into what we might call a more 'spiritual' space. From this space think about your vision. Imagine you could see beyond your own life and your own identity for a moment. What is your purpose? What are you serving in this identity as a lighthouse? A lighthouse for what? What is the vision that your mission supports?

The question here is, "What is the vision that I'm pursuing or representing as a lighthouse, and as a manager who values respect, support, skill and integrity? What vision am I pursuing as one who structures and manifests the objectives that he visualizes in his mind, takes different perspectives and maintains awareness and feedback for what is happening within himself and between himself and others? What vision am I pursuing as I am sitting, walking and listening, breathing deeply and speaking softly but clearly, standing balanced and centered, reaching out to that group of a dozen or so people in that office and those meeting rooms?"

J: (Long pause) It has something to do with congruence and integrity, but I don't know how to put it into words.

RBD: Take your time. These words are very important. There's no need to rush them. Let them emerge or flow from your unconscious. Just describe what's going on as you experience it. Maybe it's just colors or an image of some kind.

J: (Pause) I'm seeing something that looks like a vast globe or planet. The planet is mostly in the light but there are certain parts of that planet that are dark or are in the shadows. Some parts are in the shadows a lot and some are only temporarily dark. But in the times and places of darkness, people need lighthouses to help them find their way out of the shadows. I am not the only lighthouse. There are many of them, but because they are spaced just out of reach of one another to best serve the travelers, they aren't always aware that the other lighthouses are out there. But I'm hearing a kind of noise, like a fog horn, that lets the lighthouses know that other lighthouses are nearby.

RBD: (To audience) You can tell by the way that J. is speaking that this experience is a very deep one for him. Just notice how much his breathing has changed. These are experiences that we don't often open ourselves up to – except perhaps when we are near death or someone we love is near death. And yet the space for these experiences is always there in our neurology. We get so caught up in the immediacy of 'conducting' our daily lives that we forget that our daily lives occur inside of larger frameworks that are hard to describe verbally. Each of us has probably had experiences such as this, but find it hard to hold on to them or perceive their relevance in 'day-to-day' living. Yet, this is the level of experience that gives 'day-to-day' experience meaning and purpose. I believe it is possible to bring this kind of awareness into our daily work and experience.

(To J.) J., what I'd like to ask you to do is to take a moment and just be fully in the state of awareness of this planet of light and shadows, and of the lighthouses that communicate their presence to one another through their foghorns. Honor it, hold it, anchor it. And then step into your identity space and bring it with you. That's right, physically step forward to your identity space and bring this vision with you. Notice how the awareness of this larger vision strengthens and enriches your experience of who you are. If you wish, you can restate or add to your description, and metaphor, of your identity and mission.

J: I can feel it but, it's hard for me to put into words. It's like adding a kind of excitement to it all, and the awareness of being part of something bigger.

RBD: You're not just a lighthouse, there's an awareness that you are part of the light, and a network of lighthouses that provide guidance to travellers. And there's a feeling of excitement that emerges out of that vision when you bring it into your sense of identity and mission.

J: It's also a sense of being thankful...experiencing gratitude. And at the same time, it's getting much more energy.

RBD: That vision can mobilize your nervous system in a powerful way and fill it with new energy and commitment.

I'd now like to ask you to take that sense of energy and thankfulness; of being an important part of that vast planet and the network of lighthouses that bring light into dark places, and physically move forward into your belief space. Bring the sense of your vision and mission into your heart. How are your beliefs and values solidified or enriched? Would any new beliefs emerge from your heart?

J: Well, on one level, I am able to concretely feel the sense of the integrity of the whole system and the importance of relationship and support. There is also the belief that growing is good, without needing any further purpose than to grow. It is as if growth is a natural result of integrity and support. It can have a purpose, but there is a sense that growing is good even without having any purpose. That's one thing. And there is also a realization that I am supposed to be here at this time. That I also have support, and can relax, enjoy and appreciate what I am doing more.

RBD: I'd now like to ask you to focus again on that sense of being part of the vast network of lighthouses. Perhaps you can hear those foghorns in your mind as you feel your values of respect, support, skill and integrity. Also include your feeling that growing is good even if it serves no specific objective in the moment and that you belong here and can appreciate what you are doing even more. I'd like you to take all of that into your capabilities space. Connect your vision, your mission, your sense of identity and your heart to your mind. Realize that your skills and capabilities are a reflection and expression of those beliefs and values, of your identity, mission and vision. Your mind is the way in which you manifest these deep structures. As you fully sense all of these levels of yourself, how does it solidify or enrich your perception of the capabilities you have for manifesting your values, beliefs, identity and vision?

J: I have more of a capability of being in my own shoes and respecting my own point of view. Also, it's easy to see other points of view and take wider and wider perspectives. It's easier to understand other maps of the world, and other ways of thinking. It is as if I have fewer boundaries. I have more of the capability of perceiving where people and events are flowing and of giving direction to that flow.

RBD: Now I'd like to have you step forward to the behavior space and re-experience those specific actions that you take; listening, asking questions, giving verbal guidance to people from a state that is balanced and centered; reaching out to people, breathing more deeply; speaking more softly and clearly. Take this total sense of your capabilities, beliefs, identity and vision into those behaviors. Connect your strengths as a manager to your mind and to your heart and to your mission and your vision. How might you experience these activities differently? How would having this hologram of your total being enrich these very specific, concrete actions that you take? Perhaps it changes the quality of what you do.

J: It changes a lot. I am more aware of all that's going on around me, of what I'm doing and hearing. If I explain something, I have the "why" of doing it. I experience much more of a sense of confidence and meaning about my job.

RBD: Finally, I'd like to have you move back into the environment space, back to those specific 'wheres' and 'whens'; the headquarters, your office, the meeting rooms, the twelve people you interact with every day. Align your vision and sense of purpose with your identity, your heart and your mind with your actions in this environment. How would you re-perceive, re-experience and restate your sense of your environment if you brought your sense of being part of a network of lighthouses giving guidance to others into this environment? Also bring your beliefs that relationships are important and that growth is good in and of itself, your realization that you belong here at this time, your valuing of respect, support, skill and integrity. Take your ability to maintain feedback with yourself and others, to understand other maps and take a wider view, to have fewer boundaries and direct the flow of your experience. Also bring in your aligned physiology, your soft but clear voice, and the sense of awareness, confidence and meaning that you have with respect to your actions. Notice how your experience of the environment changes and enriches.

J: One difference I experience is that would be much less of doing a job. I feel like I can be much more in contact with the environment and my collaborators. I get more of the sense that I belong there. I also feel that I can be much more creative in my work.

RBD: You can also notice that this environment is a place for respect, support, skill and integrity. It is a place for wider perspectives, where different maps are understood and where growth is valued, whether it has an obvious purpose or not.

It is a place where you belong and where you can go beyond old constraints and boundaries. It is a place in which you can manifest your vision and your values.

J: Yes, I think it can be. Thank you. [Applause]

RBD: The level alignment process is something that I find to be extremely valuable. In fact, it's something that I do as a discipline on a daily basis. In the morning, for instance, as part of my preparation for being an effective seminar leader, I imagine the seminar room and how I want to act and be in my body in that room. I also review which capabilities I will need in order to be an effective leader and, which style, beliefs and values will support me most fully. I also make sure that I feel my sense of identity and mission – my purpose for being there in the first place. I then reaffirm my vision for my life's work. I then align all of these different aspects of my experience together. It often takes only about 5-10 minutes, but it's a powerful way to become ready and prepared to do my best.

Co-Alignment of Levels

The level alignment process may also be applied as a powerful way to form teams and groups. When people share a common sense of vision, mission, values and ability, they are able to work together much more effectively. This is undoubtly the basis for what is known as team 'spirit'.

The 'co-alignment' of levels between a group of people may be done as a simple extension of the level alignment process. Once each individual in a group has created an aligned state (and served as a guide for another to achieve an aligned state) the group members can get together and share their answers to the questions related to the various levels. As they listen to one another, group members would listen for the commonalities between their contexts, actions, abilities, beliefs, values, roles, missions and visions. (It is often useful to assign one person the task of writing the common answers on a flip chart.)

Once group members have shared their answers for all of the different levels and found common themes, they can synthesize their individual answers to find a 'group' vision and mission. If the group has already been formed in order to achieve a common mission or objective, members can focus on identifying their 'group' values and capabilities, etc.*

I have even used this process to help teams form a group identity by finding common values, and then considering what type of identity those values 'add up to', or are an expression of. Similar to an individual, the group would define their identity in terms of a metaphor or symbol.

The worksheet on the following pages provides an instrument for group members to use in order to identify and keep track of their responses during the alignment and co-alignment process.

---

* This process has been applied with success at companies such as Lufthansa, IBM and Fiat.

Level Alignment Worksheet

Complete the answers in the spaces provided below in order to thoroughly define the relevant areas of 'problem space' surrounding a goal or solution you would like to implement.

1. "What is the *environment* in which you want your goal or desired state?"

   "*When* and *where* do you want to enact the goal or behavior? What will be the external context surrounding the desired goal and activities?"

   In the context of

   _____

2. "What is the specific *behavior* associated with the goal or outcome?"

   What, specifically, do you want to do in that context? What is the new behavior associated with the goal?"

   I/We want to

   _____

3. "What *capabilities* are needed to reach the goal within the chosen context?"

   "*How* will you accomplish that goal and those behaviors? What capabilities and cognitive processes are needed or presupposed in order to trigger or guide those desired actions in that context?"

To accomplish this I/we will use my/our capabilities to

_____

4. "What *beliefs* and *values* are expressed by or will be validated by reaching the goal in that context?"

"What values are expressed by your goal and capabilities?"

I/We want to do this because I/we value

_____

"*Why* will you use those particular cognitive processes or capabilities in order to accomplish that goal? What beliefs provide the motivation for your thoughts and activity?"

I/We believe

_____

5. "What is your *identity* or role with respect to the goal and the beliefs and values associated with it?"

"*Who* are you if you engage those particular beliefs, values, capabilities and behaviors in that particular context?" (You may want to use a metaphor or analogy for your answer.)

I am/We are

_____

"What is your mission in that context?"

My/Our mission is to

_____

6. "What is your sense of the *larger system* in which you are operating?"

"What is your *vision* of the larger system in which you are pursuing that mission?"

This mission is in the service of the larger vision to

_____

Chapter 3

Aligning Levels of Change in a System

Overview of Chapter 3

- The Significance of Alignment in an Organization
- Levels of Change in an Organization
- Example of Failure to Align Levels in an Organization
- An Illustration of Different Levels of Process as Applied to Organizational Development
- A Framework for Effective 'Path Finding'
- 'Culture' Versus 'Cult' – Defining the Organization
- Aligning the Members of an Organization

The Significance of Alignment in an Organization

In the previous chapter we explored the importance of aligning oneself personally toward the achievement of a vision. These same principles apply to organizational development and macro leadership.

Today, many processes related to management, organizational development and leadership are undergoing a profound change for a number of reasons. In the past several decades companies have continued to become more and more complex. This complexity is a function of changes in both the internal organization of companies and their external environment. This increasing complexity has given rise to a generation of problems that were not present in the traditional company of the past.

Due to changes in technology, production methods and the workplace over the past several decades, the discretionary space of people working in companies has grown larger and larger. Especially in technologically intensive areas, people have become highly trained experts who must use their own judgment to make technical decisions (which managers themselves are not always qualified to make). Employees can no longer be viewed as 'laborers' doing a specific behavioral task who need to be watched over and controlled. As a result, the demands and skills of effective management and leadership have also become more sophisticated and complex.

Managers and leaders can no longer be effective by merely making decisions or giving orders based on their position or rank in the corporate hierarchy. Rather they must enlist the 'co-operation' and willing participation of their collaborators in order to most efficiently and effectively accomplish jobs and tasks. In order to avoid conflicts and insure optimum performance, managers must rely more on such processes as persuasion and negotiation as opposed to the processes of command or directives. In other words, as the 'discretionary space' of employees increases, the focus of the manager shifts from managing time, tasks and situations, to managing relationships and systems. Thus, *the emphasis in effective leadership and management is moving from content to process.*

Furthermore, the increasing globalization of business requires a whole different concept of management and organizational learning. The world is the company arena. Differences in cultural presuppositions, behavior patterns and values must be respected and incorporated into the daily thinking and activity of managers at all levels.

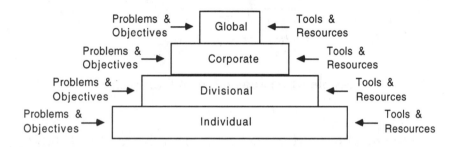

Different Levels of Objectives, Problems, Tools and Resources in an Organization

The effectiveness of a system is in many ways determined by the balance of its elements. In order for managers to congruently incorporate and coordinate different cultural presuppositions, values and contexts, these elements must be recognized and conceptualized in a way that allows the manager to effectively operate in a multi-dimensional fashion.

Alignment is a key criterion of effective planning, problem solving and leadership. In an effective system, the actions and outcomes of individuals within their micro environments are congruent with the organizational strategies and goals.

These goals, in turn, are congruent with the organization's culture and mission with respect to the macro environment.

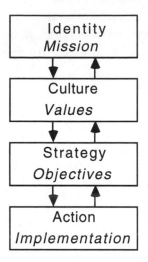

Levels of Processes in a Company

Organizations are made up of both 'hierarchical' levels and 'logical' levels of interaction. Thus, in a functional system or organization:

1) The relationship between the members of the system supports the task to be accomplished.

2) There is a shared perception of the levels, perceptual positions and time frames relevant to the problem space and solution space associated with the task.

3) There is an alignment of the various logical levels related to the task.

4) There is a congruence and alignment of the outcomes of the relevant actors involved in the system. (In a hierarchical or complementary system this is expressed through

the ease by which tasks are delegated to the appropriate roles. In a peer or symmetrical system, this is expressed through the ease by which people are able to negotiate and reach consensus about tasks and outcomes.)

5) The actions of individuals are aligned with the mission associated with their role.

In other words, there are a number of different types of alignment related to *task* and *relationship*. Types of alignment related to tasks involve:

- The professional and perceptual space of the relevant actors with the problem space to be addressed.

- The perceptual spaces of the relevant actors with one another.

- The levels involved in the task or goal.

- The levels of communication between the relevant actors.

Types of alignment related to relationship involve:

- The different levels of a person within their role.

- Levels of experience between people in different roles.

- Levels between different parts of a person.

To be effective, a leader must understand the relationship between the various levels of change, and align his or her activities to fit those dynamics. That is, *goals and actions on an individual level should support the functional objectives and strategy related to role, which in turn should be congruent with corporate culture and identity, and mission with respect to the larger environment.*

Levels of Change in an Organization

Any system of activity is a subsystem embedded inside of another system, which is itself a subsystem embedded inside of another system, and so on. This kind of relationship between systems and subsystems naturally produces different levels or hierarchies of processes. The levels of process within a social system or organization correspond closely to the levels of perception and change that we have identified for individuals and groups – i.e., environment, behavior, capability, beliefs and values, identity and 'spiritual'.

Each level of process involves progressively more of the system. Change in identity, for instance, involves a much more pervasive change (and, consequently, more risk) than a change at a lower level. It is a much simpler issue to change something in the environment or in a specific behavior than to change values or beliefs.

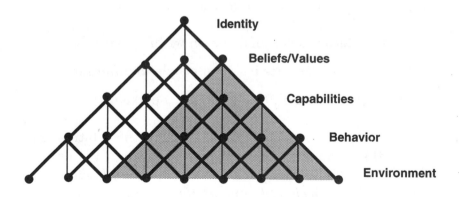

Amount of System Influenced by a Change in Beliefs and Values

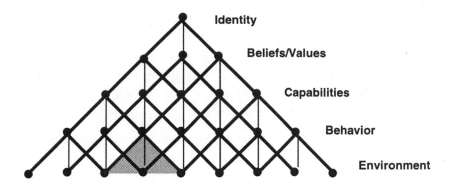

Amount of System Influenced by a Change in Behavior

It is important for leaders to recognize and address issues that may arise at any one of these levels. Consider, for example, the following statements. The various statements illustrate how interferences to completing a project could come from any one of the levels.

a. Identity: *"I am not a project manager."*

b. Beliefs/Values: *"Managing a new project is difficult and time consuming."*

c. Capability: *"I don't know how to manage a project effectively."*

d. Behavior: *"I don't know what to do in this situation."*

e. Environment: *"There wasn't enough time to complete the project."*

Leadership performance may also be influenced by issues relating to different levels. In a study on leadership interventions in an international petrochemical company (Pile, 1988), the effect of these other levels of interaction became quite clear. Managers who failed to make improvements in their leadership styles and ratings defended their lack of performance with rationalizations such as:

a. Identity: *"My role as a 'staff' person precludes me from spending time with subordinates, doing 'leadership things."* *"It would be 'carrier suicide' to change."*

b. Beliefs/Values: *"Buying people's performance is inappropriate."* *"We do not get paid for coaching and counseling."*

c. Capability: *" I don't know how to meet the requirements of my boss and at the same time meet the espoused needs of subordinates."*

d. Behavior: *"I don't know what to do to get my ratings up."* *"It takes away time from other crucial activities."*

e. Environment: *"I am not particularly worried about the results, as it is expected given what's going on. I have been in the job 4 years and am expecting a move—too bad that I will not be able to see this thing through, but the next person can do it."*

Effective leadership and organizational change requires the ability to recognize and deal with issues relating to each of these levels to some degree, in order to be completely effective. Any level that is not aligned with the others can create an interference to achieving the goals, vision or mission of the organization.

As an example, people may have been able to do something innovative (specific behavior) in a specific context but not have a mental model or map (capability) that allows them to know how to continue doing innovative things in different environments. As another possibility, even when people are 'capable' of being innovative, they may not 'value' innovation as important or necessary so they rarely attempt it. Beyond that, even people who are innovative and believe it is important do not always perceive themselves as having the role or identity of "innovators".

As with an individual, then, it is important for an organization to be aligned at all levels toward the realization of its vision.

Example of Failure to Align Levels in an Organization

A good example of the impact of the failure to align different levels is that of the Xerox personal computer.

Most readers are undoubtedly familiar with the computer mouse, but many have probably never heard of the Xerox personal computer.

Consider the following question: *"Who invented the mouse?"*

Most people think it was developed by Apple Computer. The Macintosh is sold by Apple, but Xerox actually paid something like two billion dollars developing STAR, an ancestor of Macintosh, for Apple, even though they didn't realize they were doing it.

What happened there gives you some idea of how the alignment (or lack of alignment) of levels influences a company.

In the early 1980's, John Grinder, Richard Bandler and I were doing some consulting for Xerox, and I remember seeing all these computer developments at their research center in Palo Alto. Xerox at this time was in a rather interesting position. (This will also demonstrate how powerful corporate 'programming' can be.) If you think about the identity or 'meta-program' of Xerox, it is something like, "How do I make a better copy?" This is a type of 'program' that involves "creating a match of something desirable that already exists". They make copy machines.

They had recently run into a problem though. One of their researchers walked into the Los Angeles Times newspaper headquarters and didn't see any paper in the office. There he was at a major newspaper and everybody was working with computer systems and electronic mail.

That information triggered a different 'program' than they were used to at Xerox. They started looking into the future and "matching future negatives." That is, they started imagining all of the bad things that would happen if they did not change. What happens to a company that makes its living as a result of people copying papers, and ten years in the future there is no paper in offices anymore?

So Xerox started operating "away from future negatives" and began working on all these developments in the area of personal computers.

The problem is that when you say, "Xerox," how many people think of personal computers? Most of them don't. People think of photocopies. Xerox was trying to develop these computers, but it didn't fit in with their identity, their corporate values, or even with their corporate capabilities.

They had research and development capabilities but the rest of their company was not set up to support this development in personal computers.

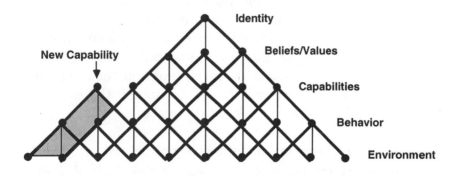

New Capability Which Does Not Fit in With the Existing Organizational Identity

We told them we thought they were trying to take too great of a leap. They were trying to create a whole new identity for themselves; but what often occurs when a company attempts that level of change is a conflict with the old identity and values. And this is exactly what happened at Xerox.

Though most people have never heard of their personal computers, Xerox did have one and tried to sell it. As a matter of fact, what happened was very interesting. It shows you the power of these belief and identity level programs and how they operate in a company.

Here are a couple of examples:

1. When they introduced these personal computers to their staff and their company, they had somebody dress up as the man who had invented the first Xerox machine. He had been dead for fifteen years or so. It seems a bit morbid to have raised him from the dead. They had him introducing this computer as the best and newest version of a Xerox machine: *"This is a better reproduction of what I tried to do."*

2. The character they used for advertising this computer was a monk! Of course, when you think of high technology a monk is not quite what comes to mind. What does a monk do? A monk sits down and copies manuscripts. Xerox was so caught in its meta-program that they did not notice that their image did not match the expectations of the people in their marketplace.

So the predecessor of Macintosh began as just an idea in their Research and Development department. At first it was no threat to anybody. It was only a little thing that people were doing at the research center. People who worked there could come in with blue jeans and long hair. At that time in the history of technology, if someone didn't have long hair and a beard, no one was really sure that person really knew what he was doing. If someone came in with a tie and was clean-shaven, they wondered if he was really capable of working with computers.

As they started investing more in this new technology and operating away from the future negative, Xerox began to develop the belief that they needed this computer technology to survive. And they tried to make it part of their identity.

As that happened, there began to be a change at the Palo Alto Research Center. The top management said, "If this is to become a serious part of Xerox, you will have to fit in with the rest of our identity: shave your beard, cut your hair, and wear a tie." They even made these people start punching a time clock – which is absurd if you know anything about technology developers.

Consider how much this mismatched the typical mental programs of the researchers. First of all, research and development people tend to have disdain for the way things have operated in the past and present and want to create something different for the future. Furthermore, these developers wanted to have their own identity, and not be swallowed up as a small part of this huge corporate identity. They wanted to be a major part of it.

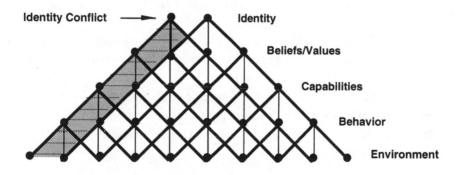

An identity conflict may occur when new capabilities and values lead to a type of identity that fails to match the present identity

So when Steve Jobs came over and said he was going to make this technology the core of Apple's identity and use it as part of a vision to change the world, what choice do you think those researchers made? Apple set up its culture to fit the working style of the researchers. Since the researchers were already in a conflict with the Xerox identity and were to become only a small part of it, when they were told that they could be the corporate symbol of Apple and Macintosh; they jumped right onto that opportunity.

The point is that in an organization you will have different types of reactions and responses as you move from one level of change to another.

We recommended that Xerox approach their situation differently – which it seems they eventually did. We advised them not to jump into personal computers, but to pace and lead their own identity; meaning to start by putting computerized enhancements on their Xerox machines.

If you are worried about not having paper in the future, then develop devices that will scan papers and digitize the words into computers instead of spending your money on making personal computers. Develop technology that will fit more with who you already are.

Xerox also eventually changed their advertising character from a monk to Leonardo da Vinci, who symbolized far greater creativity and innovation.

In summary, changes at the level of capabilty and behavior (the 'how' and 'what') frequently cause or require adjustments at the levels of values, identity and vision (the 'why', 'who' and 'who else').

An Illustration of Different Levels of Process as Applied to Organizational Development

One way to insure that all levels of an organization stay aligned, and to avoid interferences that can occur with organizational change, is through effective pathfinding and organizational development. This involves considering the relationships between the various levels as an interacting network of processes.

Consider the following hypothetical example regarding the Minerals Group of a large multinational petroleum company. The group as a whole has an 'identity' defined by its 'mission statement'. This identity is expressed in the form of core values which are connected to the key capabilities of the company. These values and capabilities determine the types of behaviors and actions undertaken by the company (such as 'digging', manufacturing', 'delivery', etc.), and the environments in which business is conducted. The relationship between these various levels could be portrayed in a diagram such as the one shown below.

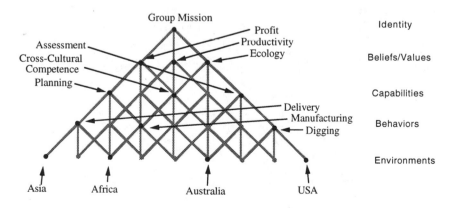

Example of Relationships of 'Nested' Levels of Processes

In this hypothetical example, the group mission would be expressed as three *'core values'* – "profit", "productivity" and "ecology". Core values would be linked to several key supporting *capabilities*, such as "planning", "cross-cultural competence" and "assessment". Specific capabilities can support more than one core value, but would tend to be closer to certain values. For instance, the capability of "planning" may support the value of "profit" more directly than would "cross-cultural competence". The capability of "assessment" may be more directly relevant to the value "ecology" than would "planning", etc.

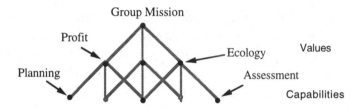

Some Capabilities Support Certain Core Values More Closely Than Others

Key capabilities would also support the specific behaviors and actions of the Minerals Group in different environments, and ensure that those behaviors were aligned to group values. "Planning" would help to ensure that "delivery" was "profitable", for example. Similarly, "assessment" would help to clarify whether "digging" was "ecological", and so on.

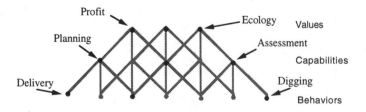

Capabilities Link Behaviors to Values

The diagram also indicates that certain behavioral concerns might relate more to certain environments. For example, 'delivery' may be more of an issue in Asia and Africa (because of difficulties in transportation) than in the USA. 'Digging', on the other hand, may be more of an issue in the USA (because of public opinion and legal restrictions) than in Asia and Africa.

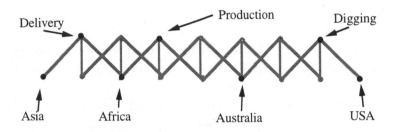

Certain Key Activities Are More Connected to Particular Environments

One strategic implication of this network concept is that the manifestation of the group mission within a particular environment would follow a particular 'path' through the network. That is, given the mission and a specific environmental/cultural location, certain 'points of tension' would be placed on various parts of the network. For example, the successful manifestation of the value of "productivity" in Zimbabwe would require certain capabilities and actions. Thus, in order to support or strengthen the commitment to "productivity" in that particular environment, changes or developments in "cross-cultural competence" and "manufacturing" may be required.

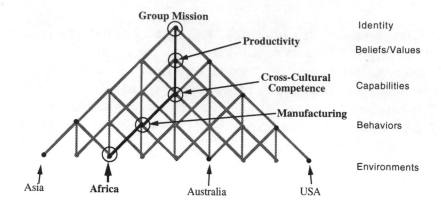

Example of 'Path' of Different Levels of Processes Required to Manifest the Group Mission in a Particular Environment

In order to achieve the desired state with respect to the group mission in some environments and cultures, multiple paths or 'points of tension' may need to be addressed – depending on the present state of that environment. In other words, it may be that, for the Minerals Group to achieve its desired state in Africa, developments in "profit", "planning" and "delivery" need to be implemented as well as support for "productivity", "cross-cultural competence" and "manufacturing".

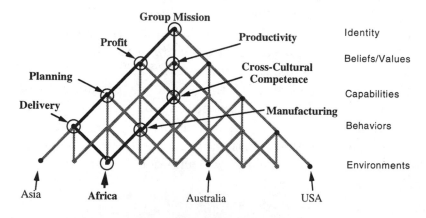

Example of 'Multiple Paths' Required for Success in a Particular Environment

Another implication of the network model is that a different set of capabilities and actions might be necessary to successfully achieve the same core value in a different environment. Thus, to achieve better profitability in the USA, a capability like "advertising" or "public relations" might be more relevant than "planning".

Furthermore, different environments and cultures would tend to require different paths or naturally bring out different 'points of tension' in the network. These different points of tension would require the strengthening or development of particular values, capabilities and/or actions to ensure success within the chosen environment.

In our hypothetical example, for instance, implementing the group's mission in the USA may require a strategy focusing more on issues related to "ecology", "assessment" and "digging" than to "profit", "planning" and "delivery".

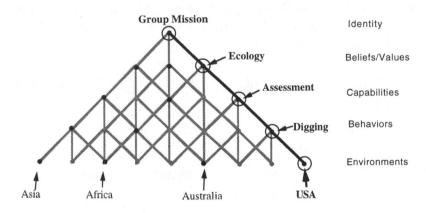

Example of Different 'Points of Tension' to be Addressed in Order to Manifest the Group Mission in Another Environment

Effective strategy formulation and 'path finding' involves taking into account the interaction and alignment of all of the various elements in this network. It also addresses the necessary 'paths' and 'point of tension' that will arise in the effort to reach the desired state in particular environments.

A Framework for Effective 'Path Finding'

'Creating a world to which people want to belong' requires the ability to find the paths to our visions and create organizations that support the movement along those paths. 'Macro leadership' skill involves establishing the paths and culture that create a "purposeful organization" capable of realizing a common vision.

According to Nicholls, "Path-finding can be summed up as finding the way to a successful future." This is accomplished through effective planning and strategy formulation.   In order to form an effective strategy or plan it is necessary to:

a) Identify the 'problem space' to be addressed. A problem space is made up of all the levels of processes influencing the state of a system.

b) Define the 'states' of movement within the problem space:

- A present state

- A goal state

- The appropriate path of transition states required to attain the goal state

c) Determine the operators (and operations) which change the states:

- To move towards the goal state

- To overcome interferences/resistance

Strategy formulation (in contrast to problem solving) begins with a definition of the Desired State. The Present State is then assessed in relation to the Desired State in order to establish the path of Transition States leading to the Desired State. The next phase in formulating a strategy involves identifying the relevant gaps and missing links between the steps in the path. A final stage involves defining the operators and operations necessary to adequately influence the Present State of the system and navigate the Path to the Desired State.

Thus, the essential framework for 'path finding' involves three basic components:

1. General definition of the Desired State and assessment of the Present State in order to determine the Gap to be covered by the Path.

2. Assessment of the key areas and levels of needs and issues to be addressed along the Path.

3. The determination of the organizational strategy and structure most likely to support the movement along the path and the manifestation of the Desired State.

For an effective strategy, the Desired State and Present State need to be assessed with respect to several key levels of processes. The **Desired State** and **Present State** worksheets on the following pages provide a tool for making a basic analysis of a Present and Desired State with respect to the relevant levels of change. These worksheets provide examples of key questions to be asked during the initial phase of 'path finding'. They may be filled out by an individual or a team of 'pathfinders' working together.

Desired State Worksheet

1. What is your Vision?

   _____

2. What is your desired Identity and Mission?

   _____

   _____

3. What are the Core Values necessary to support that
   mission (e.g., service, quality, profitability, etc.)?

   _____   _____

   _____   _____

   _____   _____

4. What are the Key Capabilities necessary to implement
   the mission and core values (e.g., research and development, planning, assessment, etc.)?

   _____   _____

   _____   _____

   _____   _____

5. What Portfolio of Activities (Behaviors) expresses and manifests your mission and values (e.g., marketing, manufacturing, delivery, etc.)?

_____   _____

_____   _____

_____   _____

6. What are the Significant Environments/Contexts in which you desire to operate (e.g., USA, Asia, Australia, etc.)?

_____   _____

_____   _____

_____   _____

Present State Worksheet

1. What is your current Mission/Identity statement?

_____

_____

In what way (if any) does the mission statement need to be adjusted or enriched?

_____

2. What are your current Core Values?

_____   _____

_____   _____

What values (if any) need to be strengthened, reprioritized or added?

_____   _____

3. What are your present Capabilities?

_____   _____

_____   _____

_____   _____

What capabilities (if any) are missing or need to be developed?

_____   _____

4. What is your current Portfolio of Activities (Behaviors)?

_____   _____

_____   _____

_____   _____

Which new actions or behaviors (if any) need to be taken?

_____   _____

_____   _____

5. What are the Significant Environments in which you currently operate?

_____   _____

_____   _____

_____   _____

What environments (if any) need to be expanded, focused upon or added?

_____   _____

_____   _____

'Culture' Versus 'Cult' – Defining the Organization

Completing the Desired State and Present State worksheets should help to provide an idea of the general 'path' to be followed to reach a "successful future", and which issues need to be addressed along the way. Once an overall path has been identified, the other aspect of effective 'macro leadership' involves "culture building". Having a strong, clear "culture" that is shared by all of the members of the organization is one of the most effective ways of avoiding the kinds of incongruencies and conflicts that can easily arise in organizations (such as the situation at Xerox described earlier in this chapter).

According to Nicholls, culture building involves "drawing people into purposeful organization – one which is capable of traveling along the path that is found or of fully exploiting current opportunities." Nicholls goes on to assert that 'culture' is built by supplying the "answers to such questions as: What is this organization all about? Where do I fit in? How am I valued and judged? What is expected of me? Why should I commit myself?" The answers to these questions come from defining the (a) vision, (b) mission, (c) path or strategy and (d) structure of the organization.

The *vision* and *mission* of the organization are the answers to the questions: What is this organization all about? and Why should I commit myself?

The *path* and the *structure* of the organization supply the answers to the questions: Where do I fit in? What is expected of me? And how am I valued and judged?

Incidentally, it is providing the answers to *all* of these questions that determines the difference between 'cult' and 'culture'. In a 'cult' (and I have seen many business cults) values and norms are imposed dogmatically from the 'top' with no explanation except that the people near the top are somehow 'closer to God'.

'Culture' is something that arises from and is shared by all the members of an organization or social system. And, while culture certainly comes from the interrelations between people 'within' an organization or social system, it is ultimately determined by that system's relationship to some larger system.

One of the biggest mistakes I have seen organizations make is failing to recognize and incorporate their relationship to something greater than themselves into their visions and mission statements. For instance, to say, "Our mission is to be a professional organization that supports and provides for our members..." is neither a mission nor a vision statement. It is at best an 'identity' statement. Mission and vision are not 'self-serving', rather they define the role of the individual or organization with respect to something beyond themselves. It is the service to something beyond the individual or organization that gives the 'purpose' to "purposeful organization."

In summary, "culture building" involves answering the following basic questions:

1. What is the larger *vision* that the organization is pursuing?

2. What is the *mission* of the organization in relationship to that vision and the community it is serving?

3. What is the *'path'* or *strategy* the organization will follow in order to fulfill its mission?

4. What is the *structure* of the organization in terms of the key tasks and relationships necceary to implement its strategy?

I have been involved in establishing a number of organizations and have used these fundamental questions as a guideline. The following are examples of 'mission statements' made for two of those organizations – the NLP World Health Community and NLP University. The NLP World Health Community is an organization that I established with my colleagues and co-authors Tim Hallbom and Suzi Smith. NLP University is an organization I created with my colleagues and co-authors Todd Epstein and Judith DeLozier.

In both cases, we got together as a team and spent several days considering the answers to these questions, not only from our own points of view but also from the perspective of potential members of the organizations and the communities they were established to serve. It was only after we had reached consensus between one another about these questions that we began to take the practical steps toward the realization of the organizations. Both of these visions are now successful international training organizations.

Example 1 – NLP World Health Community

The vision *of the NLP World Health Community is that of a global network of competent people engaged in many different areas and roles who are consistently contributing to the health and well being of others. These individuals are committed to using their strengths within their chosen vocations while sharing the common language and models of NLP.*

Albert Einstein maintained that "All means prove but a blunt instrument if they have not behind them a living spirit." An important part of the vision of the NLP World Health Community is to help transform the "blunt instruments" of medicine and health into 'tools of the spirit'.

The mission *of the NLP Health World Community is to help create more choices and alternatives for health in the world through the medium of NLP. This will be accomplished by forming a self-organizing and self-evolving network of people who share complementary missions in the area of health and who use NLP technologies and processes as their focal point. Through NLP, the members of this community can provide the "how to's," in the form of methodologies, skills and tools, to create shifts in beliefs about what is possible in the arena of health and help people develop the capabilities to mobilize and activate the natural self-healing ability within each person.*

The strategy *of the NLP World Health Community is to form and develop a core group of people who desire to be leaders within the arena of their chosen vocation – "leaders" meaning those who have the commitment* and *the skill to 'create a world to which people want to belong'. Thus, the leadership within the community will be developed through manifesting the immense range of NLP applications in the area of health and well-being.*

The structure *of the NLP World Health Community and the Health Certification Training will be like the structure of the natural healing process itself and support multiple levels of involvement. We envision the community unfolding through the establishment of international NLP health centers or institutes which will serve as focal points for the gathering and sharing of resources (such as tapes, books, articles, a computer bulletin board, research and services relating to the applications of NLP in health). The community will offer support and networking opportunities, and establish an international referral network.*

Example 2 – NLP University

The <u>vision</u> *of NLP University is to create a context in which professionals of different backgrounds can develop and contribute to both fundamental and advanced NLP tools and skills in applications of NLP relevant to their profession. The structure is set up so that individuals can focus on specific practical applications as well as attain more generalized learning.*

The <u>mission</u> *of NLP University is to provide the organizational structure through which the necessary guidance, training, culture and support can be brought to the people who are interested in exploring the global potential of Systemic NLP. This involves the encouragement of research and development in new applications, tools and models in NLP as well as providing high quality training and assessment in existing NLP skills and technologies.*

The <u>strategy</u> *of NLP University involves the diversification of NLP based trainings and materials into a number of focused application areas. Each application area is defined by the mix of 1) the kinds of NLP tools and skills to be used, 2) the kinds of people to be served and 3) the kinds of goals and outcomes to be accomplished. Thus, individuals learn practical NLP skills by developing competency with specific engineered materials related to accomplishing goals relevant to their profession.*

The <u>structure</u> *of NLP University consists of a number of interdependent courses and modules:*

1. Core courses for basic, advanced and graduate level NLP skills of approximately ten days each.

2. *Application modules which cover a variety of basic and advanced NLP applications and techniques for creativity, health, business and organizational development.*

3. *Practitioner and Master Practitioner Certification Modules consisting of a combination of core courses and application packages.*

4. *Trainer skills courses consisting of approximately ten to fourteen days each.*

5. *Individual application courses at basic and advanced skill levels.*

Aligning the Members of an Organization

According to Nicholls, the desired outcome of 'path finding' and 'culture building' is to create "committed members of the organization." Another way to facilitate this is through the co-alignment process described at the end of the last chapter. Co-alignment involves defining and identifying the areas of overlap between the various members of the system – especially those related to beliefs, values, identity, mission and vision. Similar to creating an aligned state within an individual, the basic steps of co-alignment involve:

a) Identifying the environment surrounding the project or goal.

b) Defining the behaviors to be enacted in that environment.

c) Identifying the capabilities needed in order to generate those behaviors.

d) Establishing the beliefs and values necessary to support those capabilities and behaviors.

e) Forming a description (or metaphor) for the role identity expressed by those beliefs, values, capabilities and behaviors.

f) Identifying the vision and mission that identity is 'serving'.

g) Making sure all of the different levels are connected together and are supporting one another.

Chapter 4

Creating the Future

Overview of Chapter 4

- Turning Dreams into Reality
- Dreamer, Realist and Critic
- Physiology and the Creative Cycle
- Implementing the Creative Cycle
- The Disney Planning Strategy
- Thinking Styles in Leadership and Problem Solving
- Addressing Different Thinking Styles
- Balancing Thinking Styles in a Group

Turning Dreams into Reality

Once the path from vision to action has been established, and the organizational mission, strategy and structure have been defined, the leadership challenge becomes how to navigate the path to the desired state. In my interviews with top business leaders, one of my questions involved how they managed to move to the future in the face of uncertainty and complexity. One of the leaders responded, "You certainly can't do it by trying to forecast the future. The future is much too complex and uncertain to be able to forecast."

"Then, what do you do?" I asked.

"You create it," was the reply.

A bit perplexed, I asked, "How exactly do you create the future?"

"I continually make successive approximations until I reach a point of 'no return'."

This notion of making "successive approximations" as a way to manifest a vision seems to be the essence of the strategic thinking skills necessary to achieve goals. Perhaps no one embodied this skill more completely than Walt Disney.

Disney personifies the ability to make a successful company based on constant improvement and innovation. He represents the process of turning visions into concrete and tangible expressions through organization and planning. Walt Disney's ability to connect his innovative vision with successful business strategy and popular appeal allowed him to establish an empire in the field of entertainment that has survived decades after his death.

In a way, Disney's chosen medium of expression, the animated film, characterizes the fundamental process of all effective leadership: The ability to take a vision that exists only in the imagination and forge it into a physical existence that directly influences the experience of others in a positive way.

Dreamer, Realist and Critic

One of the major elements of Walt Disney's unique genius was his ability to explore something from a number of different **perceptual positions**. An important insight into this key part of Disney's strategy comes from the comment made by one of his animators that, "...there *were actually three different Walts: the **dreamer**, the **realist**, and the **spoiler**. You never knew which one was coming into your meeting.*"

This is not only an insight into Disney but also into the process of creativity and effective planning. Any effective plan involves the coordination of these three subprocesses: dreamer, realist and critic. A dreamer without a realist cannot turn ideas into tangible expressions. A critic and a dreamer without a realist just become stuck in a perpetual conflict. A dreamer and a realist might create things, but they might not be very good ideas without a critic. A critic in the absence of a realist or dreamer is indeed just a "spoiler."

The positive purpose of the critic is to help evaluate and refine the products of creativity. There is a humorous example of a boss who prided himself on his innovative thinking abilities but lacked some of the realist and critic perspective. The people who worked in the company used to say, "He has an idea a minute...and some of them are good."

The point is that effective planning involves the synthesis of different processes or phases. The dreamer is necessary to form new ideas and goals. The realist is necessary as a means to transform ideas into concrete expressions. The critic is necessary as a filter and as a stimulus for refinement. Certainly, each one of these phases represents a whole thinking strategy all on its own – strategies that more often tend to conflict with each other rather than support each other.

The specifics of how Disney was able to methodically shift between these different strategies is something that we need to explore in more depth before we can put them into practice. For instance, how did Disney access his imagination ("the dreamer"), methodically translate his fantasies into a tangible form ("the realist") and apply his critical judgment ("the spoiler") to refine those concrete results into lasting classics?

I have examined Disney's cognitive processes in detail in my books *Strategies of Genius, Vol. I* and *Skills for the Future*. While this level of detail is not appropriate here, a significant amount of information about Disney's process of turning dreams into reality is revealed through a few key comments Disney made about his strategy.

Overview of Disney's Strategy

Perhaps the most comprehensive description of how his 'dreamer', 'realist' and 'critic' worked together comes from Disney's statement that:

> *"The story man must **see clearly** in his own mind how every piece of business in a story will be put. He should **feel** every expression, every reaction. He should get **far enough away** from his story to take a **second look** at it...to **see** whether there is any dead phase...to **see** whether the personalities are going to be interesting and appealing to the audience. He should also try to **see** that the things that his characters are doing are of an interesting nature."*

The first part of the description focuses on the interaction between the dreamer and the realist. It is clear that the "second look" is the domain of the 'critic'.

Certainly, the statement defines three distinct perspectives.

1) The 'dreamer' – vision, whole story:

> *"The story man must see clearly in his own mind how every piece of business in a story will be put."*

2) The 'realist' – feeling and action, associated, moving:

"He should feel every expression, every reaction."

3) The 'spoiler' (critic) – observer position, distant:

"He should get far enough away from his story to take a second look at it."

a) Evaluate whole project:

"to see whether there is any dead phase."

b) Evaluate individual characters and relationships:

"to see whether the personalities are going to be interesting and appealing to the audience."

c) Evaluate specific actions:

"He should also try to see the things that his characters are doing are of an interesting nature."

Disney's "second look" provides what is called a *'double description'* of the event. This 'double description' gives us important information that may be left out of any one perspective. Just as the differences in point of view between our two eyes gives us a double description of the world around us that allows us to perceive depth, Disney's double description of his own creations served to give them an added element of depth.

Of particular interest is that the "second look" involves a specific reference to being 'far enough away'. If it was too close it could be overly influenced by the other perceptual positions. Similarly, it could also overly influence them. If the spoiler is too close to the dreamer and the realist, it may inhibit the dreamer's vision and interfere with the realist's planning.

As a realist, one of Disney's major strengths was the ability to chunk and sequence his dreams into pieces of a manageable size. In fact, Disney was the innovator of the process of *story-boarding* (a process now used by all major film developers). A story-board is like a visual table of contents—it is a set of still drawings that represent the sequence of critical events to take place in the storyline of a film. Story-boarding is essentially an extension of the process of animation on a larger scale. Animation takes place through a process that involves starting with the drawing of still pictures representing the critical events of a particular movement. These drawings are typically done by the chief animator. Once the critical chunks have been defined, the individual drawings connecting these pictorial "milestones" are filled in by the secondary animation team. Disney simply extended this process of chunking and sequencing to a larger level—becoming a kind of "meta" animator.

The "story-boarding" process, which is a very powerful way of organizing and planning, can be applied to any level of the film-making procedure. From the point of view of strategy, the story-boarding process of chunking and sequencing the critical pieces required to achieve a particular result is not limited to film making and can be used for any kind of planning. It can be used to chart and organize a business project, a training seminar, a book, a counseling session, a computer program and so on.

The Steps of the Strategy

By combining Disney's comments about the thinking skills of the "storyman" with other information about his creative process, it becomes evident that Disney's process of creative dreaming primarily took place through visual imagination but also involved the overlapping and synthesizing of the senses. The dreamer focuses on the 'big picture' with the attitude that anything is possible. In general, the dreamer phase tends to be oriented towards the long term future. It involves thinking in terms of the bigger picture and the larger chunks in order to generate new alternatives and choices. Its primary level of focus is on generating the content or the 'what' of the plan or idea.

Disney's process of 'realizing' his dreams took place through his physical association into the characters of the dream and through the 'story-boarding' process of chunking the dream into pieces. The realist acts "as if" the dream is possible and focuses on the formulation of a series of successive approximations of actions required to actually reach the dream. The realist phase is more action oriented in moving towards the future, operating with respect to a shorter term time frame than the dreamer. The realist is often more focused on procedures or operations. Its primary level of focus is on 'how' to implement the plan or idea.

Disney's process of critical evaluation involved the separating of himself from the project and taking a more distant 'second look' from the point of view of his audience or customers. The critic seeks to avoid problems and ensure quality by logically applying different levels of criteria and checking how the idea or plan holds up under various "what if" scenarios. The critic phase involves the logical analysis of the path in order to find out what could go wrong and what should be avoided. The critic phase needs to consider both long and short-term issues, searching for potential sources of problems in both the past and the future. Its primary level of focus is on the 'why' of the plan.

Effective planning involves defining and managing a series of transition states leading to a goal via a feedback loop. Disney's dreamer, realist and critic cycle is an effective way to identify and navigate the path of transition states necessary to reach a desired state.

- The Dreamer stage is effective for generating and choosing the goal state.

- The Realist stage is effective for defining and implementing the path to reach the goal state.

- The Critic stage is effective for evaluating and providing feedback in relation to progress toward the goal state.

Physiology and the Creative Cycle

As with other cognitive processes, physiology is an important influence on creativity and the ability to plan effectively. There are micro and macro level behavioral cues that accompany the dreamer, realist and critic states. These cues can help you to more fully enter the 'state of mind' necessary to create a successful plan.

For instance, think about what it is like when you are 'dreaming' or in the early stages of planning a project, and are finding and exploring your options. What kinds of behavioral cues are the most significant for your 'dreaming' process? What is your posture like? Do you move around? How do you orient your head and eyes?

Now think about what it is like when you are narrowing down your options into a specific path in order to 'realize' your idea or 'dream' for a project. What kinds of behavioral cues are the most significant for your 'realizing' process? How are your movements and posture different from when you are dreaming?

Recall what it is like when you are thinking 'critically' and evaluating your plan or path. What kinds of behavioral cues are the most significant for your 'critical' thinking process?

Which of the three types of thinking styles – dreamer, realist or critic – seems to be the most natural for you?

Based on certain descriptions of Disney's behavior and the modeling of a number of different people who are effective in reaching these states, the following generalizations have been drawn about key patterns of physiology associated with each of the thinking styles making up Disney's creative cycle:

Dreamer: Head and eyes up. Posture symmetrical and relaxed.

Realist: Head and eyes straight ahead or slightly forward. Posture symmetrical and slightly forward.

Critic: Eyes down. Head down and tilted. Posture angular.

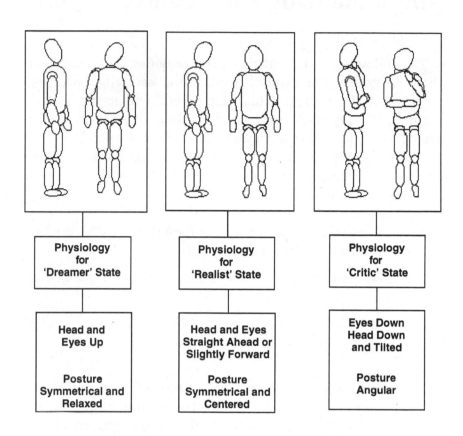

Physiology for 'Dreamer' State	Physiology for 'Realist' State	Physiology for 'Critic' State
Head and Eyes Up Posture Symmetrical and Relaxed	Head and Eyes Straight Ahead or Slightly Forward Posture Symmetrical and Centered	Eyes Down Head Down and Tilted Posture Angular

Patterns of Physical Cues Associated with Disney's Creative Cycle

Implementing the Creative Cycle

The following section of this book provides an instrument that will guide you through a planning strategy, based on Disney's creative cycle. This instrument will assist you in defining the key steps involved in implementing a particular project or vision. The purpose of the strategy is to help you develop a comprehensive plan by thinking about it from several different perspectives ('dreamer', 'realist' and 'critic'). As a result you will be able to:

a) learn an effective planning strategy that may be used in many different situations,

b) consider in detail the relevant aspects of a particular plan or project and

c) produce a document which describes the key elements of the plan or project.

Another benefit of the strategy is that you will be able to organize your thoughts more effectively and communicate them more clearly to others. It also helps you to create descriptions of projects that cover the relevant issues in a format that is comprehensive yet easy to follow.

The essential steps in the strategy involve:

1. Answering sets of questions using verbal prompts, in which the answer to the questions is already begun for you.

2. You will be taken through three sets of questions relating to different cognitive styles of thinking and planning—the 'dreamer', 'realist' and 'critic'.

3. The answers to the different question sets can then be formatted into a 'report' describing the relevant aspects of the project.

The objective of this strategy is to assist you in defining the key elements necessary for 'creating the future':

a) the overall scope of elements involved in a particular project,

b) a sequence of steps leading to the accomplishment of the project, and

c) the relevant people and 'ecology' issues relating to the project and how they will be adequately addressed by the plan.

It will also help you to understand and learn to think more effectively in each of the different thinking styles which make up the strategy.

Thus, the *'Disney Planning Strategy'* is a tool that assists you to both plan and have a means of easily recording the results of your thinking process. It also aids you in developing the flexibility to move between different styles of thinking more spontaneously.

The Disney Planning Strategy

"WANT TO" PHASE - Dreamer

> **Level of Focus:** What.
>
> **Cognitive Style:** Vision - Define the 'big picture'.
>
> **Attitude:** Anything is possible.
>
> **Basic Micro Strategy:** Synthesizing and combining the senses.
>
> **Physiology:** Head and eyes up. Posture symmetrical and relaxed.

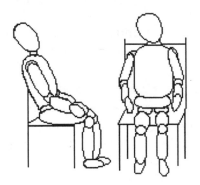

Dreamer State Physiology

State the Specific Goal in Positive Terms; Establish the Payoffs of the Idea.

1. What do you want to do? (As opposed to what you want to avoid or not do.)

The goal is to

_____

2. Why do you want to do it? What is the purpose?

The purpose is to

_____

3. What are the benefits?

The beneficial effects of this will be

_____

4. How will you know that you have them?

An evidence of these benefits will be

_____

5. When can you expect to get them?

The benefits can be expected when

_____

6. Where do you want this idea to get you in the future?

This idea will lead to

_____

7. Who do you want to be or be like in relation to manifesting this idea?

I want to be

_____

"HOW TO" PHASE - Realist

Level of Focus: How.

Cognitive Style: Action - Define the short term steps.

Attitude: Act 'as if' the dream is achievable.

Basic Micro Strategy: Associating into characters and 'story-boarding'.

Physiology: Head and eyes straight ahead or slightly forward. Posture symmetrical and slightly forward.

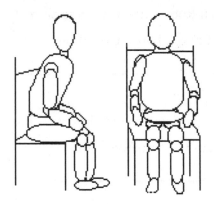

Realist State Physiology

Establish Time Frames and Milestones for Progress. Make Sure The Idea Can Be Initiated And Maintained By The Appropriate Person Or Group And That Progress Is Testable Through Sensory Experience.

1. When will the overall goal be completed?

The overall time frame for reaching the goal is

_____

2. Who will be involved? (Assign responsibility and secure commitment from the people who will be carrying out the plan.)

The chief actors include

_____

3. How specifically will the idea be implemented? What will be the first step?

The steps to reach the goal involve

(a) _____

What will be the second step?

(b) _____

What will be the third step?

(c) _____

4. What will be your ongoing feedback that you are moving toward or away from the goal?

An effective ongoing feedback will be

_____

5. How will you know that the goal is achieved?

I will know that the goal has been reached when

_____

"CHANCE TO" PHASE - Critic

Level of Focus: Why.

Cognitive Style: Logic - Avoid problems by finding what is missing.

Attitude: Consider 'what if' problems occur.

Basic Micro Strategy: Taking 'audience' perspective.

Physiology: Eyes down. Head down and tilted. Posture angular.

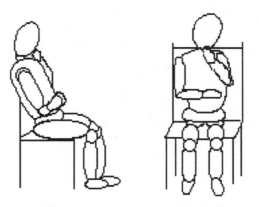

Critic State Physiology

Make Sure The Plan Preserves Any Positive By-Products Of The Current Way(s) Of Achieving The Goal.

1. Who will this new idea effect and who will make or break the effectiveness of the idea?

The people most effected by this plan are

_____

2. What are their needs and payoffs?

Their needs are

_____

3. Why might someone object to this plan or idea?

Someone might object to this plan if

_____

4. What positive gains are there in the present way(s) of doing things?

The present way of doing things

_____

5. How can you keep those things when you implement the new idea?

These positive gains will be preserved by

_____

6. When and where would you NOT want to implement this plan or idea?

I would not want to implement this plan if

_____

7. What is currently needed or missing from the plan?

What is currently needed or missing from the plan is

_____

What is a 'How' question you could ask in relation to what is needed or missing?

How _____?

Dreamer

How could you take care of what is needed or missing in the plan?

A possible solution would be

_____

Realist

How specifically can this be implemented?

This can be implemented by

(a) _____

(b) _____

(c) _____

Critic

What *else* is currently needed or missing from the plan?

What is currently needed or missing from the plan is

_____

What is a 'How' question you could ask in relation to what is needed or missing?

How _____?

Dreamer

How could you take care of what is needed or missing in the plan?

A possible solution would be

_____

Realist

How specifically can this be implemented?

This can be implemented by

(a) _____

(b) _____

(c) _____

Critic

What _else_ is currently needed or missing from the plan?

What is currently needed or missing from the plan is

_____

You can continue the dreamer–realist–critic cycle as long as you like, in order to create a type of verbal storyboard for your project or vision.

When you have finished, you can simply synthesize your answers together to form a report.

The following is an example of how simply filling in the answers to the prompts and combining them together provides the basis for an effective document describing your path and plan to reach a vision or goal. I generated this material using one of the computer tools described in the plan. The software tool guides the user(s) through the set of dreamer, realist and critic questions and collects them into a file that may be loaded into a word processor as a document.

Example – Systemic Thinking and Leadership Tools

The goal is to *create a set of multi-media tools which support effective systemic thinking, problem solving and leadership.* The purpose is to *help people develop better systemic thinking and strategic thinking abilities.* The beneficial effects of this will be *that people will be better able to define and realize their visions.* An evidence of these benefits will be *that they are able to generate enthusiasm and support for their ideas.* The benefits can be expected when *they have begun to apply the tools to their most important ideas and visions.* This idea will lead to *a greater empowerment of people involved in organizations of all types.* I/We want to be like *a lamp that illuminates the path for many travellers.*

The overall time frame for reaching the goal is *eighteen months extending indefinitely into the future.* The chief actors include *a development team and an ever widening circle of people using the tools.* The steps to reach the goal involve:

(a) *identify basic principles and strategies for effective system thinking, problem solving and leadership.*

(b) *explore the existing media and technology available for creating interactive self-learning systems.*

(c) *organize research projects which combine strategies and media to address concrete organizational problems and leadership situations.*

An effective ongoing feedback will be *that people of different thinking styles and professions will be able and willing to use the tools in their everyday work.* I/ We will know that the goal has been reached when *we have a number of cases demonstrating practical and innovative solutions as a result of the application of the tools.*

The people most effected by this plan are *the potential customers and their organizations.* Their needs are *to have more effective, less time-consuming and less expensive ways to develop practical skills and solutions.* Someone might object to this plan if *they thought it was just a useless fad.* The present way of doing things *requires no investment of time, money or effort.* These positive gains will be preserved by *creating tools that function 'intuitively' and do not demand a significant amount of time or effort to use.* I/We would not want to implement this plan if *the steps required to manifest it conflicted with the vision and values it represents.*

What is currently needed or missing from the plan is *the specific set of tools and media that need to be provided.* A possible solution would be *to draw from the existing set of systemic thinking software that I have already developed and see which ones could be most easily adapted to leadership.* This can be implemented by *selecting one or two existing tools and testing their relevance for leadership situations.*

What else is currently needed or missing from the plan is *a specific plan for the development and distribution of the tools*. A possible solution would be *to offer the tools as supplemental support to existing clients to see if they find them to be of value to develop and support effective leadership performance.* This can be implemented by *approaching colleagues who are facing specific leadership challenges and providing design examples of the tools for them to apply to their situations.*

Making a Pictorial 'Story-Board'

As a way to complete the Disney Planning Strategy, you can create a pictorial 'story-board' for your plan by finding or drawing simple images to represent the steps you have identified for reaching your vision. This can help to 'anchor' your own map of your plan and make it easier to communicate to others. Below is an example of a pictorial 'story-board' for the *Systemic Thinking and Leadership Tools* project described above.

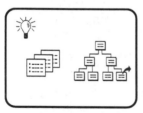 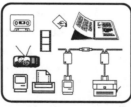 

(a) Identify basic principles and strategies for effective system thinking, problem solving and leadership.

(b) Explore the existing media and technology available for creating interactive self-learning systems.

(c) Organize research projects which combine strategies and media to address concrete organizational problems and leadership situations.

Pictorial 'Story-Board' of Systemic Thinking and Leadership Tools Project

When you have made your story-board present it to another person or a group and describe the steps in your plan. (For instance, try using it for the *Balancing Thinking Styles in a Group* exercise described on page 114.)

Thinking Styles In Leadership and Problem Solving

In addition to the 'self skills' and 'strategic thinking skills' that Disney's creative cycle provides, it also forms the basis for some important relational skills. A key consideration in leadership is how to link the 'perceptual space' of collaborators to the 'problem space' involved in manifesting a particular vision or desired state.

Effective leadership requires methods with which to typologize and manage different world views and thinking styles. The purpose of such methods is to identify and utilize different world views and thinking styles. They also help to deepen one's understanding and ability to communicate more effectively.

'Dreamer', 'realist' and 'critic' provides a typology of common thinking styles relevant to the planning context. The dreamer focuses on the 'big picture' with the attitude that anything is possible. The realist acts "as if" the dream is possible and focuses on the formulation of a series of successive approximations of actions required to actually reach the dream. The critic seeks to avoid problems and ensure quality by logically applying different levels of criteria and checking how the product performs under various "what if" scenarios. These types of cognitive styles are known as 'meta program patterns'.

Meta program patterns are an effective set of distinctions with which to analyze and identify basic styles of thinking and learning. The combinations of meta program patterns which make up a person's thinking style are an indication of how that person structures his or her map of the world as well as how that person sorts or arranges his or her experiences.

A 'program' is a cognitive process or map that guides a person's actions in order to reach an outcome. A program guides performance by collecting, chunking, comparing, assessing and ranking information. A 'meta' program is a program that operates on other programs. In other words, it determines certain characteristics in how a person thinks. Meta program patterns are descriptions of the different ways in which a problem or outcome may be approached. As with the other distinctions we have explored, a person can apply the same meta program pattern regardless of content and context. These patterns are not "all or nothing" distinctions and may occur together in varying proportions.

Meta Program Patterns

In approaching a problem or objective one can emphasize moving *"toward"* something or *"away from"* something, or some ratio of both. In a group, a problem or objective may be approached in varying degrees of proactivity and reactivity.

'Chunk-size' relates to the level of specificity or generality with which a person or group is analyzing a problem, goal or perceptual space. Concepts and situations may be analyzed in terms of varying degrees of detail (micro chunks of information) and generalities (macro chunks of information).

Problems and situations may be examined with reference to long term, medium term or short term time frames; and within the context of the past, present or future. The *time frame* within which a problem or objective is considered can greatly influence the way in which it is interpreted and approached. There might be both short term and long term implications.

Some people tend to look back at history for solutions, more than they look to the future. A good example is the difference between former Soviet leader Mikhail Gorbachev and the people who attempted to overthrow him before the breakup of the Soviet Union. One was trying to prepare for the future; the others were trying to preserve the past.

Problems and situations may be considered in relation to 'achievements' regarding the *task*, or in relation to issues involving *relationship*, such as 'power' and 'affiliation'. The question of how to balance issues relating to both task and relationship is obviously a key one with respect to leading a group. In the achievement of the task, either goals, procedures or choices may be emphasized. Issues involving relationship may be approached with an emphasis on the point of view of oneself, others or the context (the 'company', the 'market', etc.) to varying degrees.

A problem or objective may be examined by comparing for the similarities (*matching*) or differences (*mismatching*) between its elements. At the level of a group this relates to whether they are trying to reach consensus or encourage diversity.

Strategies for approaching problems and objectives may emphasize various combinations of vision, action, logic or emotion. Micro cognitive patterns on an individual level may be expressed in terms of a general *thinking style* on the macro level or group level. Vision, action, logic and emotion are more general expressions of visualization, movement, verbalization and feeling.

Meta Programs

1.
In approaching a problem one can:
• move 'away from', or 'towards', something, (or both)
• be 'proactive' or 'reactive'

2.
When a situation is being analyzed, it can be dealt with in terms of:
• details - small information chunks
• generalities - large information chunks

3.
Anything can be examined:
• within 'short-term' or 'long-term' time frames
• in relation to Past-Present-Future and combinations thereof

4.
In problem solving, aspects can be considered in relation to:
• 'Task' (the 'value' of the 'outcome')
   Choices - Goals
   Procedures - Operations
• Relationship (the 'value' of 'power' or 'affiliation')
• The points of view of:
   ⟺ Self (I, Me)
   ⟺ Other (You)
   ⟺ Context (We, The Company, The Market)

5.
A situation can be matched by identifying:
• Differences (Confrontation)
• Similarities (Consensus)

6.
One can think in terms of:
• Vision • Action
• Logic • Emotion

Some Implications of Meta Program Patterns with Respect to Leadership

It is useful for a leader to be able to identify, stimulate and utilize the different thinking styles indicated by meta program patterns. Different thinking and leadership styles are characterized by different clusters and sequences of meta program patterns in various ratios. One person's approach to a situation might involve an 80% focus on relationship and 20% focus on task, and 70% emphasis on long-term versus 30% short-term considerations. Someone else may emphasize the task as 90% of the focus and think primarily in terms of short term considerations.

The different clusters of meta program patterns clearly cover different areas of perceptual space. In this respect, there are no 'right' or 'wrong' meta programs. Rather, their effectiveness in connection with leadership relates to the ability to apply them in a way that covers the space necessary to adequately deal with a problem or objective.

Different kinds of activities require different sorts of attitudes and approaches. Some activities require or emphasize the ability to focus on the micro chunks and details. Others require the ability to see the big picture. Different phases in the cycle of a project or task may call upon different thinking styles. Therefore, particular attitudes or clusters of meta program patterns might be more or less beneficial at different stages in a project or task. An emphasis on results more than procedures might either be a help or a constraint to a group's or individual's performance at different times. Some phases of a project might require achieving consensus, yet during other phases it might be important to encourage differences in perspectives.

Thus, different thinking styles and approaches will have different values for different phases of a task or project. In the conceptual phase, for example, it may be beneficial to direct thinking in terms of the bigger picture and a longer time frame. For developing procedures it may be more useful to be focused on short term actions. For analytical tasks it may be more appropriate to logically consider details with respect to the task, etc.

In this view, managing the process of a project or group essentially involves acknowledging and directing the different meta program patterns of individuals or group members in order to fill in 'missing links' and widen the perception of problems or goals along the path from vision to action. Meta program patterns may also be utilized in order to:

1) help motivate collaborators,

2) better understand the thinking processes of collaborators and

3) help people to enlarge and share perceptual spaces.

In Summary, in relation to leadership, meta program patterns may be used to:

a. Explore the 'perceptual space' related to a particular task or goal.

b. Help to expand and enrich one's own perceptual filters and the perceptual space of others.

c. Help people to understand differences in thinking styles and to share perceptual spaces.

Addressing Different Thinking Styles

The effective management of a group involves the continual recapitulation and incorporation of the different perspectives of all group members. Thus, when leading a group, it is important to maintain a balance between a) encouraging different perspectives and b) sharing an understanding of goals and relevant issues.

Leadership situations commonly involve 1) solving problems or 2) establishing or accomplishing goals. Achieving goals and solving problems are interrelated processes that can be managed and balanced in a complementary manner. Generally, if the context is problem solving, the leader's emphasis is on encouraging new perspectives. If the context is proposing and exploring a new idea, the emphasis is on synthesizing. That is, if the group is solving a problem, the leader is seeking to promote different perspectives. If the group is implementing a new idea, the leader is seeking commonalities and consensus.

Balance is a core criterion in managing the dynamics of a group. No one stage or thinking style should be favored at the expense of the others. Various thinking styles apply differently when implementing ideas versus solving problems. For example, Dreamer, Realist and Critic are not rigid personality types, but rather are tendencies within every person. There are general strategies and purposes for different thinking styles. For example:

- The Dreamer helps to widen perceptual space related to the vision.

- The Realist's task is to define the actions necessary to realize the vision.

- The Critic's function is to evaluate the payoffs and drawbacks associated with the vision and the path to the vision.

There is a kind of dynamic balancing of processes that occurs in a group that would either be managed in such a way that different thinking styles complement one another or might result in conflict. Different thinking styles can either support each other or be quite destructive. A basic issue in managing a group is learning how to maintain that dynamic balance within the group.

Thus, an important relational skill for a leader is to be able to identify and respond appropriately to key patterns of thinking styles.

One way to elicit key information about a person's thinking style is to ask questions relating to evaluations and decision making including relationships, successes, work and discretionary time. While meta program patterns are not related to specific words, linguistic patterns serve as important cues for meta program orientation. Styles may also be indicated through non-verbal signals such as vocal emphasis, gestures and body posture.

Exercise: Balancing Thinking Styles in a Group

In this exercise, you will explore some issues relating to identifying and addressing different thinking styles:

Form a group of four. One person will be a presenter and the others will be group members.

1. Group members choose different thinking styles to role play (i.e., dreamer, realist, critic). The following table summarizes the key cognitive patterns associated with each thinking style.

	Dreamer	Realist	Critic
	What	*How*	*Why*
Representational			
Preference	Vision	Action	Logic
Approach	Toward	Toward	Away
Time Frame	Long Term	Short Term	Long/ Short Term
Time Orientation	Future	Present	Past/Future
Reference	Internal - Self	External - Environment	External - Others
Mode of Comparison	Match	Match	Mismatch

2. The 'leader' presents the plan or 'story-board' for his or her vision and manages a short discussion. The objective for the leader is to maintain a balanced interaction between the group members and keep them in a positive state.

3. After the discussion, the leader guesses the thinking styles of different group members and the group is to discuss the impact of the different thinking styles on the interaction.

Chapter 5

Managing Belief Systems

Overview of Chapter 5

- The Influence of Belief Systems in Organizations and Social Systems
- The Motivational Space of Change
- Assessing Motivation for Change
- Belief Assessment Sheet
- Bolstering Beliefs
- Basic Types of Causes
- Finding a System of Causes Through 'Connectives'
- The 'Belief Audit' – Strengthening Motivation for a Vision or Goal
- 'Belief Audit' Worksheet
- Auditing a Belief From a Different Perspective
- The Principle of 'Positive Intention'

The Influence of Belief Systems in Organizations and Social Systems

On the path from vision to action, beliefs and values are one of the most important influences. Belief in the future, belief in the possibility and capability for change, and belief in the path one is taking, are all key aspects of 'creating a world to which people want to belong.'

Beliefs and values are the non-physical framework which surround all of our interactions. Beliefs and values determine how events and communications are interpreted and given meaning. Thus, they are a key influence on motivation and culture. Shared beliefs and values are the 'glue' which holds an effective organization or team together. Beliefs and values are at the root of motivation and determine which specific strategies and actions will be reinforced or rejected. They shape how an individual 'punctuates' his or her perception of a situation. This determines which kinds of mental programs he or she selects to approach that situation and, ultimately, his or her actions in that situation.

As an analogy, consider for a moment the following words:

that that is is that that is not is not is not that it it is

At first glance, these words seem like gibberish. They have no meaning. But notice how your experience of them changes if they are punctuated in the following manner:

That that is, is. That that is not, is not. Is not that it? It is!

Suddenly, there is at least some meaning to them. The punctuation, which is on a different level than the words themselves, organizes and 'frames' them in a way that shifts our perception of them.

The words could be punctuated in other ways as well. Compare the previous punctation to the following examples:

That! That is. Is that? That is not, is not, is not! That it? It is.

That? That is!
Is that that?
Is not!
Is!
Not!
Is!
Not that!
It? It is.

The content of our experience is like the first string of words. It is relatively neutral and even void of any real meaning. Our beliefs and values determine where we place our cognitive and emotional question marks, periods and exclamation points. People don't usually argue, become depressed, or kill each other over the content in and of itself. Rather, they fight over where to place the exclamation points and question marks that give the content different meanings.

For instance, take a piece of information like, "Profits were down last quarter." A dreamer, realist and critic would perceive or 'punctuate' the exact same data in different ways, based on different beliefs, values and expectations.

Critic: Profits were down last quarter. This is terrible! We're ruined (exclamation point)!

Realist: Profits were down last quarter. We have had difficult times in the past (comma), what can we do to make ourselves more 'lean' (question mark)?

Dreamer: Profits were down last quarter. It's just a bump in the road (semi colon); we're past the most difficult phase now. Things are bound to look up.

Beliefs and values are themselves shaped by deeper level processes such as unconscious assumptions about identity, norms and culture, and by core presuppositions about the nature of people and the world. These presuppositions cannot be objectively proven but are rather taken as a matter of unquestioned faith – such as, "There is a positive intention behind every behavior;" or "All systems are inherently functional." These very basic core presuppositions are self-validating. They determine how a situation will have to be punctuated and perceived (in order to validate the core presupposition). That is, if someone is operating from the core presupposition that "There is a positive intention behind every behavior," they will continue to widen or shorten time frames, shift levels or points of view until they find the framework of perception that will validate the core presupposition.

Thus, stated beliefs and values are often derived from even deeper level assumptions about context, role, norms, etc., that are typically unstated. The beliefs which are the most influential are generally those which people are the least conscious of – like the water in which a fish swims. In organizations and other systems, beliefs are frequently not expressed overtly but rather as presuppositions in language patterns, non-verbal behaviors and 'meta messages'.

Problems often occur because people think everyone shares the same unspoken assumptions. For example, an individual might choose to send a particular type of message under the assumption that he or she is in a context of cooperation, but that message is misperceived and given a meaning unintended by the sender because the receiver assumes the context is one of antagonism or competition. Thus, beliefs and values may either be influenced directly or used as a means to uncover deeper assumptions and presuppositions.

In a functional system, beliefs and values are aligned with the organization's identity and the environment. In a dysfunctional system, beliefs undermine the larger system and can take on a life of their own, becoming a "thought virus" with a destructive capacity similar to that of a computer virus or biological virus.

Beliefs and values issues arise at different points and may either facilitate or interfere with the process of change. Clusters of common beliefs can give insight into the deeper assumptions and presuppositions upon which an organization is based. In the case of limiting beliefs, specific interventions and techniques may be devised to "immunize" against their negative potential.

Managing Beliefs and Values

As organizations change and evolve, leaders are called upon to manage the impact of those changes on the values and belief systems of the organization and the individuals who are a part of it. More and more, leaders are being required to reorganize their activity around (a) the coordination of people from different backgrounds and cultures, and (b) the implementation of values – such as 'quality', 'customer service', 'employee empowerment', etc. This brings along with it a demand for a special set of new skills and knowledge relating to the communication and management of beliefs and values.

There is a range of leadership skills necessary to address different types of belief issues. Those skills primarily have to do with perceiving and managing contexts of change and transition. The most common skills include the abilities to 'redefine', 'reframe', 'repunctuate', 'contextualize', take new perspectives and widen 'perceptual space' in order to give meaning to particular events and situations.

In general, leadership skills for managing beliefs and values are clustered around two aspects of the process of dealing with situations of change and transition: 1) perceiving change and 2) managing change. Differences in the types of skills and issues arising within contexts of change and transition depend upon the role that beliefs and values play in that context.

Some common contexts requiring leadership skill in managing beliefs and values in organizations and social systems include:

1. Situations in which new procedures, values, criteria or working relations are being introduced to replace the old ones.

2. Situations in which there are 'boundary crossings' between different groups within the organization or system (horizontal, vertical, interpersonal or interfunctional).

3. Situations involving the definition or redefinition of criteria and standards for performance.

4. Situations requiring alignment or realignment of perceptual spaces; e.g., coordination of interfunctional teams or resolution of conflicts brought about by changes imposed by top management or the environment.

The Motivational Space of Change

Leadership in organizations and social systems is needed most in situations involving change. Effective leadership skills are necessary to both stimulate and deal with the consequences of change. The basic process of change involves 1) a *person* varying his or her 2) *behavior* in order to achieve 3) an *outcome* in the environment.

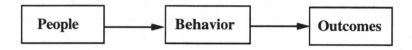

Basic Elements of Change

One important goal of effective leadership is to help people sustain interest and effort in relation to a behavioral task or objective through time in order to achieve a desired outcome or vision. This involves issues relating to incentives and motivation.

The basic motivational issues relating to change involve people a) wanting to achieve a different result, b) having the capabilities to achieve the new outcome and c) getting the chance to apply the necessary capabilities in order to attain the new result. Motivation is shaped and influenced by one's values and expectations in relation to these three issues.

1. *Desirability of the Outcome.* The degree to which a person values the consequences or results of change.

2. *Action-Outcome Expectation.* The degree to which a person expects that the skills or behaviors that he or she

is learning or engaging in will actually produce the desired benefits within the environmental system that constitutes his or her reality.

3. *Perceived Self-Efficacy*. One's degree of confidence in one's own personal effectiveness or capability to learn the skills or enact the behaviors necessary to reach the outcome.

Beliefs and expectations about the desirability of an outcome, the actions it takes to achieve the desired outcome and one's own personal capabilities play an important role in the motivation to learn or to change. For instance, a person is not likely to change his or her behavior if that person does not want to or believes he or she is incapable of doing what is required.

Such beliefs and expectations about outcomes and one's own personal capabilities play an important role in the process of organizational change. These kinds of beliefs and expectations influence how much effort people will make and how long they will sustain their effort in dealing with new or challenging situations. For instance, in self-managed activities, people who are skeptical of their degree of control over their actions tend to withdraw their efforts in situations that challenge their capabilities.

On the other hand, attaining desired outcomes through effective performance in challenging situations can help to strengthen a person's confidence in his or her existing capabilities. This is because people usually do not perform maximally, even though they possess the skills. It is under conditions that test their upper limits that people find out what they are able to do. In unchallenging situations that are 'no-brainers', even a genius will go unrecognized. Thus, by mobilizing greater effort, motivation can help to validate existing abilities, even when no new skills are acquired in the process.

According to Bandura (1982) *outcome expectancy* is a result of a person's estimate that a given behavior will lead to certain outcomes. *Self-efficacy expectation* is the conviction that one can successfully execute the behavior required to produce the outcomes.

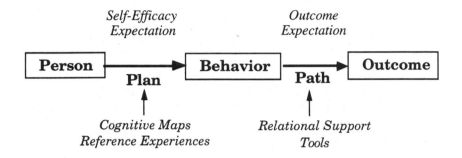

Influences on the Process of Change

In general, people change their behavior by acquiring new reference experiences and cognitive maps in order to form a 'plan'. The same behavior, however, does not always produce the same outcome. Depending on the 'path' to the outcome, the degree of relational support one receives, the amount of variability of the system and the tools one has available will determine the probability that a certain behavior will obtain a desired outcome within that system.

It is part of the task of effective micro, macro and meta leadership to provide people with the cognitive maps, reference experiences, relational support and tools necessary to establish the most appropriate kinds of assumptions and expectations to have with respect to a particular goal, task or situation.

The basic belief issues that arise in leadership in organizations relate to the fundamental components of change:

1. The desirability of the outcome.

2. Confidence that the specified actions will produce the outcome.

3. The evaluation of the appropriateness and difficulty of the behavior (regardless of whether it is believed that it will produce the desired result).

4. The belief that one is capable of producing the required behaviors necessary to complete the plan leading to the outcome.

5. The sense of responsibility, self worth and permission one has in relation to the required behaviors and outcome.

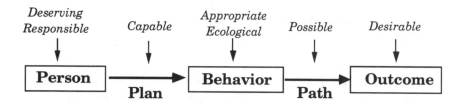

Belief Issues Related to Organizational Change

For example, let's say a leader has a vision involving "software and paper tools that will help top managers (people) make more systemic decisions (behavior) in order to improve the alignment of the activities of people within the company (outcome)." Belief issues may arise with respect to any one of the elements of change identified above.

Some people might question the *desirability* of the outcome to "improve the alignment of the activities of people within the company." Someone might argue, "Given the immediate needs that we have to improve profits, we need to focus on more urgent issues than alignment."

Others might value the outcome but question whether it is *possible* to achieve it using the proposed path. A person might say, "I don't know if it is possible to reach the level of alignment necessary given the current conditions we are facing."

Some people may desire the outcome and believe it is possible to achieve, but be unclear as to whether the behavior of "making more systemic decisions" is the most *appropriate* way to achieve the outcome. They might ask, "How will making more systemic decisions help us to better align people's actions in our current situation?"

It is also possible that people could desire the outcome, think it is possible and believe that the proposed behavior is appropriate to achieve the result, yet doubt their *abilities* to perform the required actions. They might think, "I doubt that I am capable of operating the software and paper tools well enough to actually make effective decisions."

Even when people want an outcome, trust that it is possible, believe in the actions that have been defined in order to reach the outcome and have confidence in their own abilities to perform the necessary skills and actions, they may question whether it is their *responsibility* to perform the required actions or produce the outcome. A top manager may complain, "It is not our responsibility to ensure that people's actions are aligned. That is part of their job. We are already too saturated. We don't deserve another responsibility on top of what we are already required to do."

It is also possible for people to doubt whether they in fact deserve to reach a particular desired state. Sometimes people may feel unworthy of their role or accomplishments.

These various belief issues are relevant for all levels of leadership; meta, macro and micro. They are also as important to evaluate in oneself as in one's collaborators. We are not one-dimensional beings, and often have to address our own doubts about our visions before we present them to others.

Assessing Motivation for Change

"A leader is self confident but must have doubt to create. The leader must transmit confidence and acknowledge doubt. Then transform doubt into opportunity." – Gilles Pajou

In addition to skills and actions, the underlying beliefs and assumptions of both leaders and their collaborators are extremely important in reaching their visions and 'creating a world to which people want to belong'.

On the one hand, plans and actions cannot be enacted congruently if they are in conflict with core assumptions and presuppositions of the individuals responsible for carrying them out. On the other hand, empowering beliefs and assumptions can release capabilities that are inherent in the repertoire of a particular person or group but are not being activated.

One way to determine the motivation of a person or group is to make an assessment of the five key beliefs we have identified as relevant to the motivational space of change. The beliefs can be assessed by making a specific statement of the belief as illustrated in the following examples.

1. The desirability of the outcome.

   Statement: *"The goal is desirable and worth it."*

2. Confidence that the specified actions will produce the outcome.

   Statement: *"It is possible to achieve the goal."*

3. The evaluation of the appropriateness and difficulty of the behavior (regardless of whether it is believed to produce the desired result).

> Statement: *"What has to be done in order to achieve the goal is clear, appropriate and ecological."*

4. The belief that one is capable of producing the required behaviors.

> Statement: *"I/we have the capabilities necessary to achieve the goal."*

5. The sense of self worth or permission one has in relation to the required behaviors and outcome.

> Statement: *"I/we have the responsibility and deserve to achieve the goal."*

After the beliefs have been stated, individuals may rate their degree of confidence in relation to each of the statements on a scale of 1 to 5, with 1 being the lowest and 5 being the highest degree of belief. This can provide an immediate and interesting profile of potential problem areas of motivation or confidence.

Any statements which are given a low rating indicate possible areas of resistance or interference which will need to be addressed in some way. The leader will need to provide or procure the cognitive maps, reference experiences, relational support or tools necessary to bolster confidence in areas of doubt and "transform it into opportunity."

The **Belief Assessment Sheet** on the following page provides a simple but effective instrument for quickly assessing the relevant areas of belief in relation to a goal or plan.

Belief Assessment Sheet

Write down a one-sentence description of the goal or outcome to be achieved:

Goal/Outcome: _____

Write down a short description of the current plan or solution, if any, to be enacted in order to reach the goal:

Plan/Solution: _____

_____

In the spaces provided below, rate your degree of belief in the outcome in relation to each of the statements on a scale of 1 to 5, with 1 being the lowest and 5 being the highest degree of belief.

a. "The goal is desirable and worth it."

| 1 | 2 | 3 | 4 | 5 |

b. "It is possible to achieve the goal."

| 1 | 2 | 3 | 4 | 5 |

c. "What has to be done in order to achieve the goal is clear, appropriate and ecological."

| 1 | 2 | 3 | 4 | 5 |

d. "I/we have the capabilities necessary to achieve the goal."

| 1 | 2 | 3 | 4 | 5 |

e. "I/we have the responsibility and deserve to achieve the goal."

| 1 | 2 | 3 | 4 | 5 |

As an example of how you might use this sheet, let's say a person had a vision of *"creating a computer technology that will respond to human thoughts and emotions."* To assess his or her degree of belief in this vision, the person would make the following statements and rate his or her level of confidence in each one:

"The goal to create a computer technology that will respond to human thoughts and emotions is desirable and worth it."

"It is possible to achieve the goal to create a computer technology that will respond to human thoughts and emotions."

"What has to be done in order to achieve the goal to create a computer technology that will respond to human thoughts and emotions is clear, appropriate and ecological."

"I/we have the capabilities necessary to achieve the goal to create a computer technology that will respond to human thoughts and emotions."

"I/we have the responsibility and deserve to achieve the goal to create a computer technology that will respond to human thoughts and emotions."

Let's suppose that the person has ranked his or her own belief in each statement in the following way:

Desirable and Worth It = 5

Possible = 2

Appropriate and Ecological = 4

Capable = 4

Responsible and Deserving = 3

Obviously, the belief that, *"It is possible to achieve the goal to create a computer technology that will respond to human thoughts and emotions,"* is the area of greatest concern. It is here that the leader would first want to focus his or her attention to find the cognitive maps, reference experiences, relational support and tools to strengthen his or her own beliefs and expectations, before presenting this vision to others.

If this leader was working with a team of others, it would also be valuable and important for the leader to assess the beliefs of that team with respect to the vision. Identifying common areas of doubt would point to key areas of concern. And, if there are differences in the rankings of the various beliefs, the individuals who have greater confidence may have information or reasons that can help to raise the expectations of others.

Bolstering Beliefs

The purpose of our beliefs is to guide us in areas where we do not know reality. That is why beliefs have such a profound influence on our perceptions and visions of the future. To manifest a vision, we must believe that it is possible for something to occur even though we are not certain that it will happen. If we were certain of the future, we would not require leadership.

We build and strengthen our beliefs based on the cognitive maps, reference experiences, relational support and tools that we have available to us. These form the 'reasons' why we believe something in the first place. In order to bolster our own belief in a vision or to influence the beliefs of others, we must identify 'good reasons' why someone should believe in that vision. The more reasons that we have to believe in something, the more likely it is that we will believe in it.

One important relational and strategic skill of leadership involves the ability to identify and articulate the reasons to believe in a particular vision or to participate in a particular mission. This involves finding and supplying the answers to several important "why" questions, such as:

Why is it desirable?   *Why is it possible?*
Why is this the appropriate path?
Why am I/are we capable? *Why are you/we responsible?*

According to the Greek philosopher Aristotle, answering these types of questions would involve finding the underlying 'causes' related to the various issues. In other words, we must discover:

a) what causes it to be desirable
b) what causes it to be possible
c) what causes this to be the appropriate path
d) what makes me/us capable
e) what makes you/me responsible

Basic Types of Causes

According to Aristotle (*Posterior Analytics*) there were four basic types of causes: 1) "formal" causes, 2) "antecedent," "necessitating" or "precipitating" causes, 3) "constraining" or "efficient" causes and 4) "final" causes.

Formal Causes

Formal causes essentially relate to fundamental definitions and perceptions of something. The "formal cause" of a phenomenon is that which gives the definition of its essential character. We call a bronze statue of a four-legged animal with a mane, hooves and a tail a "horse" because it displays the form or 'formal' characteristics of a horse. We say, "The acorn grew into an oak tree," because we define something that has a trunk, branches and a certain shape of leaves as being an 'oak tree'."

Formal causes actually say more about the perceiver than the phenomenon being perceived. Identifying formal causes involves uncovering our own basic assumptions and mental maps about a subject. When an artist like Picasso puts the handlebars of a bicycle together with the bicycle seat to make the head of a 'bull' he is tapping into 'formal causes' because he is dealing with the essential elements of the form of something.

This type of cause is related to what Aristotle called "intuition." Before we can begin to investigate something like success, alignment or leadership, we have to have the idea that such phenomena might possibly exist. For instance, identifying 'effective leaders' to model implies that we have an intuition that these individuals are in fact examples of what we are looking for.

Seeking the formal causes of a problem or outcome, for instance, would involve examining our basic definitions, assumptions and intuitions about that problem or outcome. Identifying the formal causes of "leadership," a "successful organization" or "alignment" would involve examining our basic assumptions and intuitions about these phenomena. What exactly do we mean when we talk about our "leadership" or about "success," an "organization" or about "alignment?" What are we presupposing about their structure and their "nature?"

Antecedent Causes

Antecedent, necessitating or *precipitating causes* relate to those past events, actions or decisions that influence the present state of a thing or event through a linear chain of 'action and reaction'. This is probably the most common form of causal explanation that we use to describe things. For instance, we say, "The acorn grew into an oak tree because the man planted it, watered it and fertilized it." "Gandhi became a leader because of his bitter experiences of color discrimination in South Africa." Or "This organization is successful because it took those particular steps at those particular times."

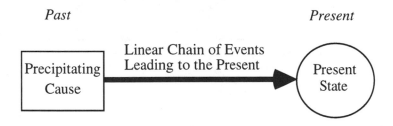

Antecedent or Precipitating Cause

Seeking the precipitating causes of a problem would involve looking for the chain of events in the past that lead to the present state of the problem. Similarly, seeking the antecedent causes of a desired state would involve looking for the linear cause-and-effect chain which will bring it about.

Constraining Causes

Constraining or *efficient causes* involve ongoing relationships, presuppositions and boundary conditions (or lack of boundaries) within a system which maintain it's state (regardless of the chain of events that brought it there). For instance, applying this kind of cause, we might say, "The acorn grew into an oak tree because there was no significant competition for water and light from the trees surrounding it." "Gandhi became a leader because his personality fit the needs of the society in which he acted." "The organization was successful because it had no real competition."

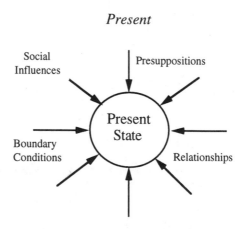

Efficient or Constraining Causes

Identifying constraining causes would involve examining what holds a particular phenomenon's current structure in place, regardless of what brought it there. For instance, in exploring the constraining causes of an organization's success we would examine the current constraints or lack of constraints that could cause an organization to fail or suddenly take off, regardless of its history.

Seeking the constraining causes of a problem or outcome would involve examining the conditions surrounding the problem or outcome, such as the prevailing social conditions and other influences which might stabilize or destabilize a certain situation. Constraining causes tend to be more 'systemic' in nature, and may be defined in terms of potential constraints which were not present as well as those which were.

Final Causes

Final causes relate to future objectives, goals or visions which guide or influence the present state of the system giving current actions meaning, relevance or purpose. Final causes involve the motives or 'ends' for which something exists. In this sense, final causes often relate to a thing's role or 'identity' with respect to the larger system of which it is a part. In his biological researches especially, Aristotle focused on this type of causation - the intentional aim or end of nature - which he held to be distinct from the 'mechanical causes' also operative in inorganic phenomena.

He noted that, if one burns an acorn, he destroys it in a mechanical way but that, if he gives it a chance, it turns *itself* into an oak. Thinking in terms of this kind of cause we might say, "The organization was successful because it was driven by a powerful vision." "Gandhi was an effective leader because he stayed focused on his ideals of peace and harmony." "The team was aligned in their actions because they shared a common goal."

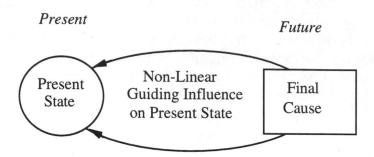

Final Cause

Seeking the final causes of a problem or outcome would involve considering the intended goals, purposes and desired results that are directing or restricting the thoughts and actions of the individuals involved in the outcome or problem situation. It would also involve considering the individuals' perceptions of their own identity within the environmental and social systems that they are operating.

In summary, attempting to find the *formal causes* of a problem or outcome leads us to view it as a function of the definitions and assumptions we are applying to the situation. Looking for *precipitating causes* leads us to see the problem or outcome as a result of particular events and experiences from the past. Seeking *constraining causes* leads us to perceive the problem or outcome as something brought out by ongoing conditions within which the current situation is occurring. Considering *final causes* leads us to perceive a problem or outcome as a result of the motives and intentions of the individuals involved.

Finding a System of Causes Through 'Connectives'

In our language, Aristotle's different types of causes are reflected in certain key words known as 'connectives'. Connectives are words or phrases that link one idea to another; such as:

because	*before*	*after*
while	*whenever*	*so that*
in the same way that	*if therefore*	*although*

We relate ideas together through these 'connective' words. For instance, if we were to say "Gandhi was an effective leader," and follow it with the word "because" we would be lead to identify some 'cause' which brought us to our conclusion. As an example, we might say, "Gandhi was an effective leader *because* he congruently embodied his vision and mission through his actions."

Different connective words can be used as a means to explore or 'audit' the various 'causes' related to a particular phenomenon. One simple method is to pick a problem or outcome and then systematically go through each of the connectives listed above to find any relevant associations, assumptions or beliefs. For example, if we wanted to explore or 'audit' the system of causes related to a symptom such as 'a drop in productivity', we would start with a statement of the problem or symptom such as "Productivity is decreasing." Holding this problem statement constant, we can go through each connective to explore the total 'space' of causes related to that symptom.

a) To explore precipitating causes you would want to use the words *"before"*, *"after"* or *"because."*

b) To explore constraining causes you can use the words *"while"* or *"whenever."*

c) To explore final causes you can substitute the phrase *"so that"* or *"therefore."*

d) To explore formal causes you can try the words *"in the same way that"* or *"if."*

e) To explore potential counterexamples and constraints in order to check the strength of your cause-effect premises you can substitute the word *"although."*

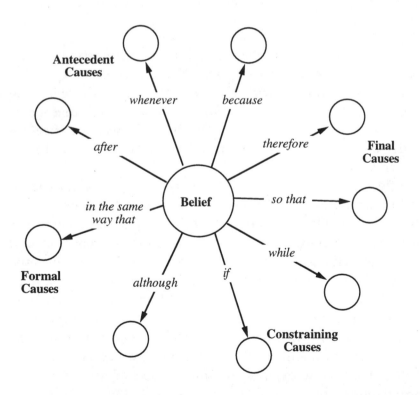

System of Causes Addressed by 'Connectives'

The following statements provide an example of how the method would be applied to the symptom of decreasing productivity.

Productivity is decreasing *because*

_____

Productivity is decreasing *therefore*

_____

Productivity is decreasing *after*

_____

Productivity is decreasing *while*

_____

Productivity is decreasing *whenever*

_____

Productivity is decreasing *so that*

_____

Productivity is decreasing *if*

_____

Productivity is decreasing *although*

_____

Productivity is decreasing *in the same way that*

_____

This same process could then be repeated with the statement of the outcome to explore and audit the desired state. Thus, if our outcome statement is, "I/we want to improve productivity," we would hold this statement constant and repeat the cluster of connectives:

I/we want to improve productivity.

because _____

therefore _____

after _____

while _____

whenever _____

so that _____

if _____

although _____

in the same way that _____

Resources for reaching the desired state may be identified by altering the outcome statement slightly and repeating the process. Instead of saying, "I/we want to improve productivity," we can say:

I/we will improve productivity

because _____

therefore _____

after _____

while _____

whenever _____

so that _____

if _____

although _____

in the same way that _____

The 'Belief Audit' – Strengthening Motivation for a Vision or Goal

Motivation and confidence may be strengthened by applying a process similar to the 'cause audit' described in the previous section. For example, an individual or group may choose a particular belief and systematically go through each of the connectives to find any other related supporting associations, assumptions or beliefs.

For example, if there were a question as to whether the individual or group possessed the capabilities necessary to achieve the goal, the process would start with the statement of that particular belief: "I/we have the capabilities necessary to achieve the goal." Holding this belief statement constant, individuals would then go through each connective to explore a broad 'space' of supporting reasons.

In this case it would be important to begin each new sentence prompted by the connective with the word "I" or "we". This helps to insure that the individuals remain associated in the experience and avoid merely making 'rationalizations'. Thus, the series of new statements would be created in the following manner:

e.g.
I/We have the capabilities necessary to achieve the goal
because I/we

_____

I/We have the capabilities necessary to achieve the goal
therefore I/we

_____

I/We have the capabilities necessary to achieve the goal *after I / we*

_____

I/We have the capabilities necessary to achieve the goal *while I / we*

_____

I/We have the capabilities necessary to achieve the goal *whenever I / we*

_____

I/We have the capabilities necessary to achieve the goal *so that I / we*

_____

I/We have the capabilities necessary to achieve the goal *if I / we*

_____

I/We have the capabilities necessary to achieve the goal **although I / we*

_____

I/We have the capabilities necessary to achieve the goal *in the same way that I / we*

_____

After finishing the new statements, it is interesting to read each of the entries deleting the prompt words – with the exception of "although". (It is important to retain the word "although" or that particular response will appear negative.) The series of responses can form a surprisingly coherent and valuable statement of reasons to have confidence in the belief.

As an example, let's return to the hypothetical situation we were exploring for the Belief Assessment process. We had concluded that the belief, *"It is possible to achieve the goal to create a computer technology that will respond to human thoughts and emotions,"* was the one which was accompanied by the most doubt. Applying the Belief Audit process would involve repeating this belief and adding different connectives to the end of the statement. Filling in the blank created by adding the connectives serves to widen the 'perceptual space' related to the vision and 'reframe' possible interferences. The process is illustrated in the following example:

It is possible to achieve the goal to create a computer technology that will respond to human thoughts and emotions **because I/we** will discover what is necessary as we make successive approximations.

It is possible to achieve the goal to create a computer technology that will respond to human thoughts and emotions **therefore I/we** can begin the path to the vision with confidence.

It is possible to achieve the goal to create a computer technology that will respond to human thoughts and emotions **after I/we** complete a thorough study of leading edge 'mind-body' technologies.

It is possible to achieve the goal to create a computer technology that will respond to human thoughts and emotions **while I/we** keep in mind that we must be open to several different perspectives and variables.

It is possible to achieve the goal to create a computer technology that will respond to human thoughts and emotions **whenever I/we** keep our focus on the desired outcome and stay open to the issues and opportunities that arise along the path to realizing it.

It is possible to achieve the goal to create a computer technology that will respond to human thoughts and emotions **so that I/we** <u>can make a tremendous technological breakthrough.</u>

It is possible to achieve the goal to create a computer technology that will respond to human thoughts and emotions **if I/we** <u>look to the deeper principles and don't get caught up in the details at the beginning.</u>

It is possible to achieve the goal to create a computer technology that will respond to human thoughts and emotions ***although I/we** <u>do not yet know what the final form of the technology will be.</u>

It is possible to achieve the goal to create a computer technology that will respond to human thoughts and emotions **in the same way that I/we** <u>have accomplished many things in our lives without consciously knowing the specific steps we will take before we start.</u>

At the end of the audit process you can group the belief statement together with the answers generated by the audit process to create a paragraph.

> *It is possible to achieve the goal to create a computer technology that will respond to human thoughts and emotions. We will discover what is necessary as we make successive approximations. We can begin the path to the vision with confidence. We will complete a thorough study of leading edge 'mind-body' technologies. We will keep in mind that we must be open to several different perspectives and variables. We will keep our focus on the desired outcome and stay open to the issues and opportunities that arise along the path to realizing it. We can make a tremendous technological breakthrough. We will look to the deeper principles and won't get caught up in the details at the beginning.*

Although we do not yet know what the final form of the technology will be, we have accomplished many things in our lives without consciously knowing the specific steps we will take before we start.

As you can see, this creates a coherent set of ideas that can help to strengthen confidence in the belief. The paragraph defines elements of a pathway to the vision, provides motivation and addresses possible objections. Because the group of statements identify a multiplicity of reasons (or causes) for confidence and puts them into words, it becomes an important document for the leader and the group. It can provide the leader with an overall explanation justifying confidence in the vision. It also provides a rich source of ideas for addressing doubts and for "transforming doubt into opportunity."

'Belief Audit' Worksheet

1. Review the ratings you gave the various beliefs on the Belief Assessment Sheet that you completed earlier. Write down the belief you want to strengthen in the space marked 'Belief' below.

2. For each of the 'prompt' words below, repeat the sentence expressing the belief. Then add the prompt word(s) and complete the sentence with whatever 'spontaneously' comes to mind.

3. When you are finished, redo the belief assessment process and notice what has changed and been strengthened.

Belief:_____

because I / we

_____

therefore I / we

_____

after I / we

_____

while I / we

_____

whenever I / we

_____

so that I / we

_____

if I / we

_____

* although I / we

_____

in the same way that I / we

_____

As you try this process with one of your own beliefs, you will realize that some of the prompts are easier to respond to than others. You may also find that it is easier or more appropriate to respond to the prompts in a different order than they are listed. Of course you can feel free to answer the prompts in the order that feels most natural and comfortable for you or your group, and it is okay to leave some of the prompts blank. I have found however, that the prompts which seem most difficult to answer often lead to some of the most surprising and insightful results.

Auditing a Belief From a Different Perspective

Sometimes it is difficult or unfruitful to audit a belief from your own perspective. In fact, doubts often arise because we are stuck in our point of view and cannot see any other choices.

Another way to use the Belief Audit process is to do it while considering the vision and belief from the shoes of another person. This can open new 'perceptual space' and help to remove unconscious blocks to creativity. It can also help you to find unconscious or unnecessary assumptions.

This form of the Belief Audit can be done by identifying a person, either actual or hypothetical, who *does* have full confidence in the particular belief you have doubts about. Then you, or some other group member, can step into the shoes of that person and 'role play' his or her responses to the various prompts. To facilitate the role play, you would want to use the word "you" instead of "I" when initially responding to the prompts.

To test the influence of the other perspective on your own confidence level, you can then repeat the responses generated by the other perspective substituting the word "I" for "You". It often helps to have another person read the responses to you first, so you can get a sense of the statement from both perspectives.

For example, if the statement generated from the role-played perspective is *"It is possible to achieve the goal to create a computer technology that will respond to human thoughts and emotions* **because You** <u>have the motivation and experience necessary to translate that vision into reality,</u>" you would repeat the response in first person. That is, you would say, "I" or "We have the motivation and experience necessary to translate that vision into reality."

'Belief Audit' Worksheet 2

Follow the steps listed below and use the worksheet on the next page to help you audit one of your beliefs from another person's perspective.

1. Review the ratings you gave the various beliefs on the Belief Assessment Sheet that you completed earlier. Write down the belief you want to strengthen in the space marked 'Belief' on the following page.

2. Associate into the perceptual position of someone that does have confidence in that belief—i.e., someone who believes in you and your vision.

3. For each of the 'prompt' words, repeat the sentence expressing the belief. Then add the prompt word(s) and complete the sentence with whatever 'spontaneously' comes to mind, as you stand in the 'shoes' of that person. Use the word "you" when addressing yourself.

4. Return to your own perspective, and have someone stand in the position of the person who believes in you and read each of the sentences you have generated (leaving out the 'prompting' words except for "although").

5. Repeat each sentence, as they are being read to you, substituting the word "I" for "you."

6. When you are finished, redo the belief assessment process and notice what has changed and what has been strengthened. (Another belief assessment sheet has been provided at the end of this section.)

Belief:_____

because You / I

_____

therefore You / I

_____

after You / I

_____

while You / I

_____

whenever You / I

_____

so that You / I

_____

if You / I

_____

* although You / I

_____

in the same way that You / I

_____

Belief Assessment Sheet

Write down a one-sentence description of the goal or outcome to be achieved:

Goal/Outcome: _____

Write down a short description of the current plan or solution, if any, to be enacted in order to reach the goal:

Plan/Solution: _____

In the spaces provided below, rate your degree of belief in the outcome in relation to each of the statements on a scale of 1 to 5, with 1 being the lowest and 5 being the highest degree of belief.

a. "The goal is desirable and worth it."

| 1 | 2 | 3 | 4 | 5 |

b. "It is possible to achieve the goal."

| 1 | 2 | 3 | 4 | 5 |

c. "What has to be done in order to achieve the goal is clear, appropriate and ecological."

| 1 | 2 | 3 | 4 | 5 |

d. "I/we have the capabilities necessary to achieve the goal."

| 1 | 2 | 3 | 4 | 5 |

e. "I/we have the responsibility and deserve to achieve the goal."

| 1 | 2 | 3 | 4 | 5 |

The Principle of 'Positive Intention'

One of the most important and useful principles for managing belief systems relates to the notion of 'positive intention'. This principle is especially valuable when dealing with limiting beliefs. The principle essentially states that: *At some level, all behavior is intended or has been developed for some "positive purpose".* According to this principle, for instance, resistances or limiting beliefs would actually emerge from some underlying positive intention or purpose. For example, the positive purpose behind the belief, "It is not my responsibility to motivate my collaborators," may be to 'protect' the speaker from oversaturation or failure. The positive intention behind a belief such as, "It is not possible to align the actions of everyone in the organization," might be to prevent 'false hope' or to avoid unrewarded effort.

The principle of positive intention implies that, in order to successfully change a resistance or limiting belief, these underlying concerns, or positive purposes, must be acknowledged and addressed in some way. The positive intention behind a resistance or limiting belief may be addressed directly or by widening the person's map of the situation such that they are able to see choices for satisfying their positive intent other than resistance or interference.

In fact, resistance created by positive intentions often arise from other limiting (and unrecognized) assumptions. For instance, the reason that a person may feel threatened by the "responsibility to motivate collaborators" may be because that person does not feel he or she has the skills or support to successfully fulfill the responsibility. This concern may be addressed by supplying training and coaching along with the new responsibility. Another way to address this might be to help the person realize that he or she already has the capabilities necessary and is going to be supported.

The principle of positive intention is derived from the deeper assumption that *the map is not the territory*. In other words, there is a difference between our experience of the world and the world itself. We make our personal maps of the reality around us through the information that we receive through our senses and through how we connect that information to our own personal memories and experiences. Therefore, we don't tend to respond to reality itself, but rather to our own mental maps of reality.

From this perspective, there is no one 'right' or 'correct' map of the world – especially when it relates to parts of reality that are unknown or have not yet happened, such as the future. We all have our own world view and that world view is based upon the mental maps that we have formed. It's these internal maps that will determine how we interpret and react to the world around us. Our model of the world gives meaning to our behaviors and our experiences more so than 'objective' reality. Thus, it's generally not external reality that limits us, constrains us or empowers us, rather it's our map of that reality.

From this perspective, people make the best choices available to them given the possibilities and capabilities that they perceive to be accessible within their model of the world. Processes such as the Belief Audit are one way to help people widen their map of a situation and perceive other choices and options. It is also important at times to consider or inquire directly about the positive intention or purpose behind a particular resistance or limiting belief.

Thus, when managing an objection brought up by a collaborator, it is useful to begin by acknowledging the collaborator's positive intent and then lead to a wider space of perception or thinking. It is especially important to separate a person's identity and positive intention from their behaviors. In dealing with interferences, an effective strategy is to first acknowledge the person or their positive intent and then respond to the issue or problem as a separate issue.

It is important to realize that one can acknowledge another person's point of view without having to agree with that person, i.e. it is different to say "I understand that you have this perspective", than to say, "I agree with you". Saying, "I appreciate your concern", or "That is an important question" is a way to acknowledge the person or their intention without necessarily implying that their map of the world is the right one.

Appendix A provides a description of how you can apply these principles in order to overcome resistance by acknowledging a person's point of view and then shifting to higher levels of criteria and values.

In summary, according to the principle of positive intention, when dealing with resistance to change it is important and useful for leaders to:

1) Presuppose that all behavior (including resistance and limiting beliefs) is positively intended.

2) Separate the negative aspects of the behavior from the positive intention behind it.

3) Identify and respond to the positive intention of the resistant/problem person.

4) Offer the person other choices of behavior to achieve the same positive intention.

Processes such as the Belief Audit can help by:

• Reframing the problem or goal by taking a different point of view.

• Shifting the 'level' of focus.

• Identifying limiting (but unrecognized) assumptions.

• 'Chunking down' to set sub goals, or addressing partial areas of perceptual space.

• Encouraging "as if" thinking.

Chapter 6

Effective
Communication

Overview of Chapter 6

- Communication and Relational Skills in Leadership
- The Communication Matrix
- Monitoring Internal States
- Managing Meta Messages
- Pacing and Leading
- Representational Channels and Thinking Styles
- Basic Perceptual Positions in Communication and Relationships
- The Skill of Meta Communication
- Practicing Effective Communication Skills

Communication and Relational Skills in Leadership

Once you have identified a vision, a pathway to the vision, a plan to navigate the path and the relevant belief issues related to navigating the path, it is then time to begin moving along the path. This involves specifying and communicating the necessary goals and tasks to be accomplished and managing the relationships between the people involved in carrying out those tasks within the organizational system. This is the arena of micro leadership.

Effective micro leadership involves the application of practical communication and relational skills that are essential for expressing oneself and accomplishing goals while working together with others. These skills make it possible for a leader to create contexts in which people can thrive and excel.

Effective communication and relational skills involve:

1) An understanding of people's subjective experiences.

2) A set of principles and distinctions to recognize patterns in people's behaviors and thinking styles.

3) A set of operational skills and techniques that influence people's behaviors and thought patterns.

Communication and relational skills support effective leadership by allowing the leader to foster communication and understanding between people in order to help them more effectively accomplish their tasks. These skills are a function of how a leader uses verbal messages (both spoken and written) and non-verbal messages (ranging from visual aids to his or her own voice tone and gestures) in order to facilitate understanding, address different thinking styles and encourage participation and effective performance.

The Communication Matrix

The *communication matrix* provides a simple but useful model of communication. This model can help you to both understand the process of communication better and to develop more effective communication skills.

According to the communication matrix, communication involves people sending messages to one another through various media. Thus, the three basic elements involved in any process of communication are: 1) *people*, 2) *messages* and 3) the *medium* through which the messages are being sent.

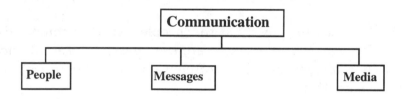

Basic Elements Involved in Communication

People

The simplest case of communication, for instance, would involve two people sending and receiving messages from one another through the medium of the spoken word. The two would alternate at various times between (a) the 'sender' or 'transmitter' of various types of messages and (b) the 'receiver' of various types of messages from the other. As the two people interact, in addition to spoken language, they may at times also draw diagrams, make gestures or refer to written material as a medium for the various messages they are attempting to transmit.

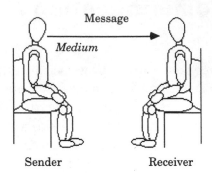

A 'Sender' Transmits a Message to a 'Receiver'

People - Physical Dimensions

As we look more closely at the 'people' aspect of communication, we can consider that there are physical, internal and relational dimensions that influence their communication with one another.

On a physical level, a one-to-one communication may be expanded to a one-to-a-few (e.g., a leader to a team) or a one-to-many (e.g. a presenter to an audience). This will influence the types of messages being sent and received and the media through which those messages are being sent. Communication also happens between few-to-few (e.g. one group or team to another), few-to-one (e.g. a committee to a CEO) and few-to-many (e.g. a board of directors to shareholders). Likewise, there are communication situations involving many-to-many (e.g. a nation to a nation or one organization to another), many-to-a-few (e.g. a group of voters to their representatives) and many-to-one (e.g. a class to a teacher).

Each of these variations in the physical dimension of the people involved in communication will influence the types of messages and media through which the communication is occurring (i.e., memos, phone calls, reports, newspaper articles, e-mail, television, films, books, etc.).

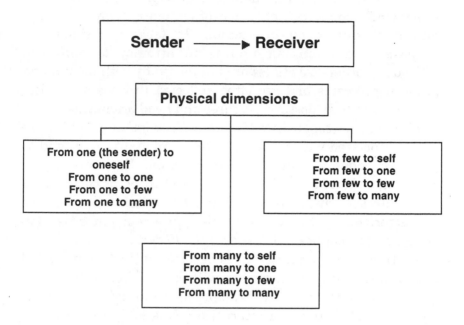

It is important for a leader to take into account this physical dimension of communication and recognize the value and need for the different types of media and messages for each condition. While a leader is most often in the situation of one-to-one, one-to-few or one-to-many, effective leadership sometimes involves the other combinations as well.

People - Internal Dimensions

The internal aspect of people that most influences communication is their *state*. The internal states of both sender and receiver impact the flow of the communication. States act as both a filter and a bias in receiving and interpreting messages. A person's internal state is typically a function of his or her attitude and thinking style.

Attitudes, such as "confidence," "concern," "openness," "enthusiasm," "curiosity," etc., are often more temporary and may shift during an interaction. In fact, sometimes the purpose of a communication is to attempt to shift the attitude of others. Attitudes are influenced by both mental and physical processes and are often reflected in certain physical cues, such as body posture, gestures and head orientation.

Thinking styles, such as 'dreamer', 'realist' and 'critic', are more associated with an individual's personality and tend to be more constant during an interaction. Rather than be changed, different thinking styles need to be acknowledged and addressed in some way. Different thinking styles are characterized by the various 'meta program patterns' discussed in the chapter on *Creating the Future*.

Attitudes and thinking styles determine the 'chemistry' of the interaction; i.e., whether it will be volatile, stable, sluggish, etc. In addition to recognizing and managing his or her own internal state in an interaction, it is often essential for leaders to take into account the states of others. Communicating to a group of 'concerned critics' can be quite different from communicating with a group of 'enthusiastic dreamers'. And, depending upon one's outcomes, both present their own unique challenges.

People - Relational Dimensions

The relational dimension of people involved in a communication has to do with their roles or *'status'* with respect to one another. In organizations and social systems, issues of 'status' can be quite influential and also fairly complex at times. There are several fundamental types of status: complementary, symmetrical and reciprocal. A *'complementary'* relationship is one in which the role of one person "complements" that of the other - such as subordinate to boss, a student to a teacher or a child to a parent. Complementary relationships are often a function of organizational or social hierarchies.

'*Symmetrical*' relationships are essentially peer relation-ships, in which people are in similar roles and treat each other as 'equals'. '*Reciprocal*' relationships are those in which the people involved periodically "pass the baton" or trade roles during the interaction. In a team interaction, for instance, individuals may trade off "leading" the team at various times. Thus, in a reciprocal relationship, individuals may at various times be "boss", "subordinate", "teacher", "student", etc.

There is one other basic type of "status" that is relevant in leadership situations, which could be called *"meta-comple-mentary"*. A meta-complementary relationship is like that of a consultant to a client. On the one hand, the consultant is "working for" the client (in this sense the client is the "boss"). On the other hand, however, the consultant's job is to direct the behavior of the client (in this sense the consultant is the "boss" in certain ways).

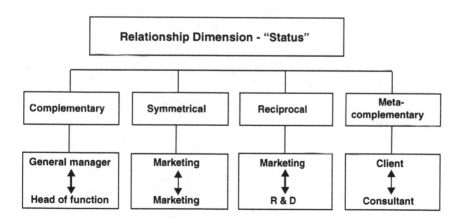

Different types of messages and media are often used to acknowledge and adapt to different types of status. Many languages, for example, have both a formal and familiar version of the word "you" to acknowledge the difference between complementary and symmetrical relationships. Other verbal acknowledgments of relationships involve the use of words like "sir" or "madam" and the use of a person's last name or first name to establish 'status'. Similarly, different media are often used to acknowledge different types of status. A phone call indicates a different type of status than a formally written document or a letter sent by courier.

'State' and 'status' are also important to consider together during a communication interaction. For instance, it is quite a different situation for an enthusiastic subordinate to communicate to a skeptical boss than for an enthusiastic boss to communicate to a skeptical subordinate.

Messages

Intended Versus Received Messages

In considering the 'message' element of communication, a first distinction needs to be made between the 'intended' message and the 'received' message. In NLP there is a saying that "the meaning of your communication is the response you elicit; regardless of what you intended to communicate." In other words, the 'meaning' of a message to the receiver is what that individual 'receives', irrespective of the intent of the sender. This statement is an acknowledgment that the message intended by the sender is not always the message that is received by the others involved in the interaction. One of the most important communication skills of leadership is insuring that the message you intended is the one that was received. As one of the leaders in my study maintained, "The challenge is to get people to do what you wanted, not what you said." In essence, effective communication is a feedback loop between sender(s) and receiver(s) which attempts to optimize the congruence between the intended and received messages.

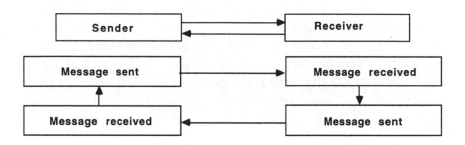

Feedback Loop Between 'Sender' and 'Receiver'

Received messages are often influenced by the state and status of the receiver. It is important for leaders to have a certain degree of observational skills in order to detect cues indicating shifts in the state and status of 'receivers'.

Messages – Micro, Macro and Para

In considering the components that make up a particular communication, it can be useful to distinguish between 'micro messages', 'macro messages' and 'para-messages'. Micro messages relate to the details of the communication and involve messages containing specific ideas or steps. A micro message would be like a particular sentence in a paragraph. Macro messages have to do with the ability to get across a general idea. Typically, a 'macro message' is composed of a series of micro messages (like the relationship between a sentence and a chapter in a book).

Para-messages relate to the fact that several messages may be sent simultaneously. A 'para-message' is a message that accompanies another message. Para-messages are usually sent through a different channel than the primary message. Pointing to something with your finger while you are talking about it is an example of a non-verbal para-message.

A para-message may support another message or contradict it. For example, when a person says, "I would like three coffees please," and simultaneously holds up three fingers, his or her para-message is congruent with the verbal message. On the other hand, if a person says, "I think that is a good idea" but is simultaneously shaking his or her head "no," the para-message is conflicting with the verbal message.

Messages and Meta messages

This leads us to the relationship between the 'content' of a message and the 'meta message'. The content of a message is generally accompanied by higher level 'meta messages' (often non-verbal) that give emphasis or provide cues for how to interpret the message. In many cases, the 'content' relates to the purely verbal aspect of the communication, while meta messages relate to the non-verbal portion of the communication. Meta messages are messages *about* other messages. In this sense, meta messages are a special form of para-messages. While para-messages may contradict the primary message, meta messages are on a different 'level' than the content. As an example, a leader may tell a group to "Pay attention" while pointing to his or her eyes. This gesture would be considered a "meta message" indicating *how* the group is to pay attention (i.e., by watching). If the leader were pointing to his or her ears, it would indicate a different mode of paying attention.

Using a yellow highliter to mark out key phrases in a text is another example of a meta message. Punctuation also serves as a meta message. Changing a question mark to an exclamation point, shifts the meaning of the rest of the message. Even the medium through which a message is sent can be a meta message. A message sent by fax or courier would indicate an urgency with respect to task. A phone call or personal meeting would place an emphasis more on the relational aspects of the message contents.

The function of a meta message is basically to inform the listener as to what 'type' of message is about to be delivered or has been delivered, and how to best 'receive' that message. In other words, meta messages are necessary in order to 'decode' the 'meaning' of a message. Thus, the same message will have different meanings if accompanied by different meta messages.

As an analogy, when one computer is communicating with another it needs to send certain 'control characters' along with the actual text it is transmitting. The control characters are meta messages informing the other computer what kind of data it is sending and where to place it in its memory.

Levels of Messages

The purpose of meta messages is often to clarify at which 'level' the content of a message has been sent or received. As an example, if a leader gives a collaborator the verbal message, "You made a mistake," it could be interpreted in several different ways. Is this message intended to be focused at the level of identity or behavior? In other words, is the leader indicating disappointment in the person or simply giving feedback about a particular action? This type of information is often critical for the proper interpretation of a communication. Clearly the message "you made a mistake" takes on a completely different meaning if the meta message is "I want to help you do better" than if the meta message is "I am angry at you."

Such information is often communicated through non-verbal cues such as voice inflection. The statement, "*You* made a mistake," is more likely to be interpreted as an indication that the collaborator has done something wrong and is in trouble. The statement, "You made a *mistake*," on the other hand, would be more likely to indicate an emphasis on an event or the correctness of a procedure rather than the person.

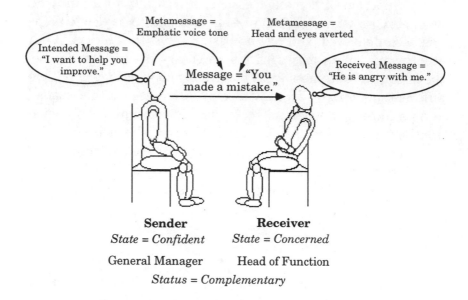

Sender
State = Confident

Receiver
State = Concerned

General Manager   Head of Function

Status = Complementary

Elements Influencing the Type of Message Received

Because meta messages are typically communicated non-verbally, they are often outside of the awareness of both the sender and the receiver. Developing the awareness to read and monitor meta messages is probably one of the most essential micro leadership skills.

Other Types of Meta Messages

In addition to clarifying the level of a message, meta messages may communicate information about:

1) The state of the sender or receiver.

2) The status of the sender or receiver.

3) The type of context in which the communication is taking place.

Micro physical cues, such as body posture, voice tone and tempo, eye contact, etc., are indications of both state and status. Two people sitting side by side looking at a report would be a meta message about a different type of state and status than if one person is sitting with his or her arms folded while the other is walking about the room in an agitated manner.

Certain behaviors are also meta messages about context. Wearing a suit and tie, for example, indicates a certain formality in a context. When a person takes off his jacket and tie, and rolls up his sleeves, it is a meta message that the context has shifted somewhat and that it is time to get "down to work".

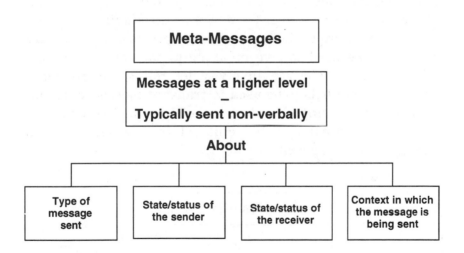

Types of Meta Messages

Media

Clearly, all messages must be transmitted through some kind of medium. The various media through which a message can be conveyed have different constraints and strengths which influence how the message is sent and received. In organizations, the medium through which a message is sent is made up of:

1) the channel of communication,

2) the context of the communication,

3) the cultural framework surrounding the communication.

Channels of communication are related to the different sensory modalities by which a message may be represented. The context and cultural framework surrounding the communication relate to the types of assumptions and inferences which will be used to give meaning to the communication. Effective communication involves determining the sequence and mix of channels to be used to transmit messages. It also involves considering the meaning of the various channels within the context and the cultural framework in which messages are being sent.

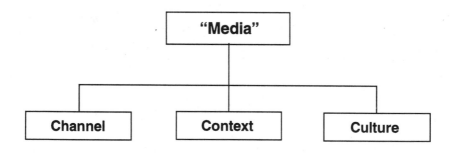

Elements Forming the 'Medium' of a Message

Media - Channels

Channels of communication are related to the different sensory modalities by which a message may be represented. Our abilities to communicate and understand messages come from our capability to make maps in our minds. We build our mental maps out of information from the five senses or 'representational systems': sight, sound, feeling, taste, and smell. Our senses constitute the form or structure of thinking as opposed to its content. Every thought that you have, regardless of its content, is going to be a function of pictures, sounds, feelings, smells or tastes, and how those representations relate to one another. We are constantly linking together sensory representations to build and update our maps of reality. We create these maps based on feedback from our sensory experience.

"Representational channels" relate to the senses and the type of sensory modality or representation a person is using to either send or receive a message. When someone is speaking out loud he or she is using a verbal channel of external representation. A more visual or symbolic form of external representation would involve drawing or displaying symbols and diagrams. Similarly, when a person is receiving a communication he or she may be more focused on sights, sounds or feelings. Thus, the selection of the channel of communication may be made based on the thinking style and focus of attention of the receiver.

The basic types of representational channels involved in communication are:

- Verbal

- Written

- Pictorial

- Physical

Different modalities of representation have different strengths. The verbal mode of representation, for instance, has a lot of strengths in terms of how information is sequenced with respect to logical dependencies. The visual channel is often the best way to synthesize information into a whole or 'gestalt'. Acting out an idea or concept physically brings out its concrete aspects.

Emphasizing different channels of communication and representation can lead people into different types of thinking styles. For example, the visual channel helps to stimulate imaginative thinking. The verbal channel is often most effective for logical or critical thinking. Focusing on physical channels influences people toward an action orientation.

Different representational channels can also influence people's relationship to information. For instance, writing something down on a flip chart is a simple way of encouraging consensus, because once an idea is expressed on paper the person who proposed the idea is not so intimately associated with the idea anymore. Externalizing an idea allows you to separate the *what* from the *who*.

Media - Context

'Context' is another important aspect of the medium in which messages are sent. As an illustration of the influence of context on communication, consider the following scenario:

A husband and wife are sitting on the sofa in their living room watching television. At a certain moment the wife turns to the husband and asks, "Are you cold?" Without saying a word, the husband gets up from his chair, shuts the window and then returns to his seat.

How do you explain what has happened here? If he were to have responded only to the verbal message of his wife, the husband would have simply answered her question "yes" or "no." Instead, the husband interpreted the meaning of his wife's words within a wider context of both physical and non physical aspects of the situation.

The physical dimensions of a context have to do with external cues and constraints. For instance, the husband's response in the scenario described above was influenced by the fact that the window was open and he was sitting together with his wife on the sofa. If the window was already closed and the husband had just put on his coat and was getting ready to run an errand, he probably would have responded to his wife's words in a different way.

If someone enters a room that is set up with a blackboard at the front and chairs arranged facing the front of the room in "theater style," he or she is likely to interpret it as a context for a 'presentation' and be prepared to sit passively and listen. If that person enters a room in which a small group of chairs is arranged facing each other in a "round table" format, he or she will most likely interpret it as a context for 'discussion' and be ready to be more proactive and participative. This type of influence is referred to as the "psycho-geography" of the situation.

Time constraints are also an important contextual influence. For example, if a time limit of 15 minutes has been set for a meeting, it is more likely that the meeting will be interpreted as being task oriented rather than as an exploratory brainstorming session.

The non-physical dimensions of a context have to do with parameters such as people's goals, roles, the phase of work they are in, etc. A meeting with a defined objective of "team building" creates a different context than a meeting with the defined objective of "planning" or "reaching consensus" about a course of action.

Media - Culture

As the example of the husband and wife demonstrates, communication is often given meaning based upon unspoken assumptions and presuppositions. In order to make sense out of a particular message or experience, one must make assumptions about the situation in which one is operating. Different assumptions influence the priority and relevance one gives to elements of a message or experience. We have explored the influence of beliefs and assumptions in detail in the previous chapter. From this perspective, it is important to consider what is presupposed by one's own messages and messages of others.

Context and culture determine, and are determined by, the kinds of assumptions and expectations people apply to a particular situation. 'Culture' is also embodied in both overt and unspoken rules. 'Rules' establish constraints and reflect beliefs, values and assumptions. Rules define what is appropriate and inappropriate in a particular context or situation. Different cultures have different assumptions and rules about the significance of time, space, attire, etc. Being 10 minutes late for a meeting in one culture, for instance, might be perfectly acceptable. In another it could be considered as a serious transgression. Cultural rules and assumptions can even influence people's perceptions of reality. A German acquaintance of mine, for example, was riding in a car with a colleague from Spain. As they were approaching a stop light, it turned red. The German rider was terrified and appalled when his colleague drove through the red light without even slowing down. "Didn't you see that the light was red?" she exclaimed. Her driver replied, "Yes, but it was only a little bit red."

Rules relate to both context and status. For example, in some cultures direct eye contact is the only way to show that you are truly paying attention. In other cultures it is considered disrespectful or insulting. Obviously, being aware of cultural influences as part of the medium of communication is an important leadership skill, especially in situations involving trans-cultural interactions.

Communication Strategies

'Communication strategies' relate to managing the mix of elements defined by the communication matrix.

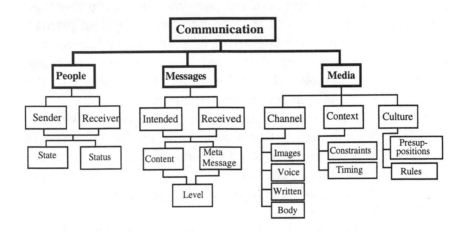

Elements of the Communication Matrix

There are several classes of activities related to one's communication strategy:

1) Determining the general message and 'chunking' it into the content elements and meta messages.

2) Establishing the current and desired state, status and context in which the messages and meta messages are to be sent.

3) Determining by what channels message and meta message elements will be most effectively transmitted.

4) Recognizing and responding to feedback about how messages and meta messages are being received by others.

A communication strategy involves elements which are preplanned and aspects which are selected or adopted in response to feedback. The preplanned aspects of a communication strategy essentially relate to how information is prepared and delivered. For example, having the same message in a written report and on a transparency is a meta message about the significance of the information. Whether printed material is given at the beginning of a meeting or handed out during the progression of the meeting is a meta message about how to perceive that information with respect to the other information that has been presented.

The dynamic aspect of managing messages involves the continuous monitoring of how messages are being sent and received – i.e., the ability to adapt one's messages and meta messages according to the responses received as reactions to other messages. Messages may be 'adapted' via:

1) Using observational skill and feedback to reduce distortions between intended and received messages.

2) Determining the selection and combination of messages and meta messages.

3) Ensuring that the micro messages support the larger message and lead in the direction of the communication outcome.

The following sections of this chapter will explore different aspects of the communication matrix in more detail, emphasizing how they may be synthesized into an effective communication strategy.

Monitoring Internal States

Managing one's own internal state and the states of one's collaborators is one of the most important and influential skills of micro leadership. Non-verbal cues are often one of the most relevant and influential aspects of monitoring and managing internal states. It is important to acknowledge the influence of behavior, even very subtle aspects of physiology, on communication. Different states or attitudes can be expressed through different patterns of language and behaviors. In this sense, states are often influenced by meta messages and are themselves a meta message about what sort of information is being sent or received. That is, if someone suddenly shifts from being open to being skeptical, it is a meta message about how that person is receiving your messages.

Physiology also provides a powerful leverage to change people's states and thinking processes. Physiological cues give us tools to influence internal states as well as the cognitive processes associated with effective communication.

As a leader, it is important to realize that in situations in which you experience stress or conflict, you might express those attitudes even though you're not aware of it. As you become aware of these kinds of cues, some of them become more obvious, especially in situations where people are acting spontaneously.

A core skill for an effective communication is to recognize the connection between behavioral cues and patterns on the one side, and attitudes and thinking styles on the other. To accomplish this it is important to have the skill to distinguish between 'observation' and 'interpretation' when interacting with others. *Observation* involves simply noticing patterns of behavioral cues. *Interpretation* involves giving meaning to what one observes.

To say that someone "is sitting with his arms folded" is an observation. To say that someone "is closed to new ideas" is an interpretation of those cues. While that interpretation may be accurate, it is important to know that it is a personal judgment, and to recognize how one arrived at that judgment. This is because sometimes people misread or misinterpret non-verbal meta messages. In fact, one of the distinguishing characteristics between cultures is the variation in their use and interpretation of non-verbal cues.

It can be difficult to appreciate the differences in the micro physiology related to different states unless you are very accurate in your observation because many behaviors appear to be similar. This kind of accuracy involves a certain commitment to observation which you may not always have time for in daily life. On the other hand, there might be certain contexts where it's worth the investment of precision. For example, detailed observation may be essential in certain intense interactions or in very delicate situations. As one of the leaders in my study commented, *"There are moments where a leader has to have the ability to change the second half of his sentence based on the feedback he received in response to the first half of the sentence."* Not that you would always do that, but sometimes circumstances require that degree of commitment to observational skill.

Having sensitivity to the non-verbal aspects of communication allows the leader to recognize and encourage states in others. One method for accomplishing this is called "shaping". Shaping has to do with encouraging something in a physiological way. For example, there is a story about a psychology professor who conducted an experiment with a group of university students. He instructed the students in his class to compliment or non-verbally express approval for women who wore red sweaters. They were not to comment on the sweater itself but just to say something like, "Oh, you look nice today," or to smile at them. Supposedly, after a week, he walked into the dining hall and it was filled with women in red sweaters.

Apparently the students also decided to try the process on the professor himself. If the professor went to one side of the room when he was teaching, the students all agreed amongst each other to yawn and act bored. If he went to the other side of the room, they all sat up, nodded their heads and acted very interested. After a while the professor found himself doing all of his teaching from one side of the room!

Managing Meta Messages

The process of 'shaping' involves the use of verbal and non-verbal 'meta messages' – messages ABOUT other messages. In face-to-face communication meta messages are most often transmitted non-verbally. People are constantly sending meta messages, even when they themselves are not talking. Linguists call this the 'grunts and groans' phenomenon of communication.

When people are listening they are often making noises like "Ah," "Uh huh," "Hhmmm," etc. As it turns out, these noises are not just random. They are meta messages about how they are receiving the messages being sent. If somebody is rapidly going "Ah ha, ah ha, ah ha," for instance, it indicates he or she is receiving the message differently than if that person slowly says, "Ahhh haaaa."

I once modeled a top manager at IBM who almost exclusively (though unconsciously) used meta messages to direct people to 'discover' that they agreed with his approach. When he was talking with somebody that was thinking along similar lines as he was, he was a wonderful and very active listener, constantly making eye contact, nodding his head and saying things like, "Oh really?" "That's interesting." "Tell me more about your idea." If somebody started to go off in a direction he didn't like, he would stare blankly and mumble "Uh huh...Uh huh." It was like talking to a brick wall. As soon as the other person began to shift directions, the manager would come back to life and become very interested in the other person's direction of thinking. People found themselves eventually coming around to his way of thinking without understanding why.

As I mentioned earlier, the same message will have different meanings if accompanied by different non-verbal meta messages. For example, consider the difference in the implications of the following messages:

"You should not try to think *that way* at this time."

"You *should not* try to think that way at this time."

"*You* should not try to think that way at this time."

Based on the placement of voice inflection, the message takes on different implications relating to a particular level of emphasis:

> *You* (identity) *should not* (beliefs/values) *try to think* (capability) *that way* (specific behavior) *at this time* (environment).

It is the presence or lack of such meta messages that often determines how a message is received and whether or not a message will be interpreted appropriately.

For example, if a leader says "YOU weren't respecting the rules," this is much more likely to be taken as an identity message. If the leader says, "You weren't respecting the RULES," then he or she is not emphasizing the individual identity so much as the level of *what* and how.

Thus, a typical non-verbal communication skill is the ability to use voice stress. If a leader says, "Now I want you to pay close attention to what I will say next," in a monotone voice he or she will probably not accomplish the intended purpose of getting the group's attention. The same message with a different voice stress as a meta message would give it a different meaning. The leader could say, "I want you to *pay close attention* (with voice emphasis) to what I'm going to say next." That non-verbal aspect of the communication will have an influence on how people receive that message.

People in companies and organizations are often exposed to so much information that a key question for them is what to emphasize or what's important. This is typically done through the non-verbal meta messages that accompany the information.

Somebody even experimented with the influence of meta messages in relation to the computer. One of the problems with a computer is that it doesn't give meta messages. So, they decided to program the computer to give meta messages to the people who were using it. The computer would constantly print responses like, *"Oh yes." "I see." "Very good."* It turned out that people really liked using this computer! They were actually more productive with the computer because they somehow felt more rapport with the computer, even though they couldn't tell you why.

Different kinds of meta messages are used in different ways in different cultures. For example, someone once did a study on the interactions between people in English pubs and people in French bistros. They found that the French touched each other on the average of approximately 110 times per hour. The English touched each other only an average of three times per hour.

Meta messages do not only relate to voice stress. They come from many other non-verbal aspects of communication. In addition to voice inflection, some other ways in which a leader sends non-verbal meta messages are through gestures and the movement of his or her body. Setting up the meeting room in a certain way is a meta message about the kind of interaction that you want people to have.

The geographical relationship between group members has an important non-verbal influence upon group process. It often has both a physical and symbolic influence on shaping the interaction between group members. For example, sitting in a circle, as in a round table, encourages different types of feedback and interactions between group members than sitting at a rectangular table or in a 'theater style' arrangement. A round table also conveys a different kind of symbolic relationship between group members. This influence is called 'psychogeography'.

Pacing and Leading

If you have ever watched people communicating, you have probably noticed that, at times, they tend to imitate each other. When people interact and begin to establish rapport with one another, frequently there's a matching of certain behaviors that starts to occur. They will begin to sit in a similar posture, speak at a similar rate and in a similar tone, and even take on similar gestures. This is related to a process called "pacing" in NLP. If you watch people carefully, you will notice that when two individuals are really in rapport with each other, they do a lot of mirroring of each others' behaviors. This is a basic principle of communication that can be used as a tool to help lead people more effectively.

Pacing is the process of using and feeding back key verbal and non-verbal cues from the other person, in order to match his or her model of the world. It involves having the flexibility to pick up and incorporate other people's vocabulary and behavior into one's own vocabulary and actions. The process is important to many of the essential aspects of effective communication, (such as rapport and trust building). When you are pacing, you are trying to step into another person's shoes and experience their model of the world. In pacing you want to communicate with someone in their own language and through their own way of thinking.

For instance, one way to develop rapport is by listening to the kinds of language patterns a person uses and then doing a type of "active listening" by matching some of their words. So if somebody says, "I *feel* that we need to go more deeply into this," you might say, "Yes, I understand that you have a *feeling* that we need to explore this."

Of course, it is easier to 'pace' people you already know and with whom you already have rapport. It's like a meta message acknowledging your rapport in that case. But in situations involving people that you're not familiar with, it might be difficult; and it might even be disrespectful. On the other hand, it can be a very effective way of encouraging rapport with people with whom you are unfamiliar. One suggestion in that situation would be to do it in stages so that you pace one element at a time. You might begin by matching the other person's voice tone and then respectfully adding body posture, gestures, etc.

Leading involves the attempt to get another person to change, add to or enrich his or her behavior or thinking process by subtly shifting one's own verbal and behavioral patterns in the desired direction. The basic idea of pacing and leading is to incrementally introduce somebody to changes in their behavior or world view by first matching and acknowledging, and then widening their model of the world. For instance, when people are being introduced to something new, it is best to start with something familiar and then move to something new.

Most people think of leadership as being primarily associated with 'leading'. But often the most effective leaders are those who can first understand and respect other people's models of the world, and have the flexibility to incorporate those other world views into their own visions. In other words, effective leadership requires effective 'pacership'.

A good example of the power of pacing before leading comes from a sales seminar for a telemarketing group. There was one customer that no one had been able to sell to. It turned out this person talked very s...l...o...w...l...y. However, he was the president of a big company that could become a very important customer. People would call him and say, "Hello, sir, I know you're a very busy man, if I could just take a minute of your time," speaking at about twice his speed.

But that isn't the way that person thinks, or listens. As a way to improve his communication skills, a member of the group was instructed to call this man up and say, "Hello... (very slowly)... I'm from xxx company... and I'd really like to have some time... to talk with you.... when you really have some time... to think about our products... I know it's really important for you... to take your time and think about things... Could you tell me when we could call...." and so on. Instead of saying, "I'll only take a minute." You say, "When could I call you back when you would have enough time to think about this comfortably and thoroughly?" The company president felt so comfortable with the approach that he scheduled a meeting, and the telemarketing group ended up getting the account.

As this example illustrates, one of the most important outcomes of pacing is the establishment of rapport. When people know you can think as they do and can take their world view into account, they are much less resistant to new ideas.

There are a lot of ways of pacing someone. In addition to matching voice tone and tempo, you can match key words and physical posture. One way to pace someone at a very deep level is to speak at the rate which the other person is breathing. You speak in tempo with their breathing rate.

This can even help in dealing with problem people. For example, once during a presentation on communication skills I was giving, a man stood up and said, "All this stuff you are saying about communication seems too easy. I'm in the REAL WORLD. These theories are only for seminars. I just don't feel that it will work with MY clients." So I said, "You certainly have a legitimate concern. Why don't you come up and be a demonstration subject? You pretend that you're one of your difficult clients in the real world, and we'll try to get a hold of how this might put you more in touch with them."

So he came up and started "role playing." The first thing I did was to subtly put myself into a similar body posture. He said, "Well, I'm a busy man. I have to see a hundred people like you every day. Most of them are full of crap and end up wasting my time. Let's hurry up and get through this." As I responded to him I began to match my speech to the man's breathing, and said, "It sounds to me... like you want some-one... you feel you can trust... Someone who cares.... about what you need... and will support you...Think of somebody you have really trusted... in your life... and how you felt... That's the kind of relationship... I'd like to develop with you." I continued pacing his breathing, and finally after about three minutes of this the man stopped him and said, "You know, I was going to try to be as resistant as I could, but right now I'd buy anything from you."

This example illustrates the value of using simple but subtle non-verbal cues to help establish rapport and to pace and lead another person's state so that they are more open to 'receiving' your messages.

Leadership and Rapport

One of the most important relational skills of leadership is the ability to establish rapport with one's collaborators. The quality of performance you can draw out of others will be greatly influenced by the amount of rapport you have with them. People generally experience more rapport with people who share a similar model of the world.

Matching language patterns is one way of acknowledging someone else's model of the world. Identifying and incorpo-rating key words, micro metaphors and examples commonly used by a particular individual or group is another way of sharing their maps of the world and attaining rapport.

Pacing or subtly mirroring their non-verbal communica-tion can also greatly enhance their experience of rapport because they will perceive you as being "like them". Some ways to non-verbally pace or mirror people include putting yourself into a similar body posture, using similar intonation patterns and expressions, dressing similarly, etc. This is a powerful form of putting oneself 'into the shoes' of another person.

Representational Channels and Thinking Styles

To be an effective leader, it is critical to keep in mind that *everybody has his or her own map of the world.* When a person wants to communicate something or understand something, that person will construct a mental map of the idea or concept. It is the job of the leader to recognize (and in some instances to help develop) the thinking styles of their collaborators and to provide as many options and choices as they can that will fit those styles.

People's maps of the world are constructed from experiences they perceive through their sensory representational systems. People will often find themselves more at home with one sense than the others as they build their mental maps. For some people "seeing is believing;" others rely much more heavily upon their feelings; whereas other people value what they hear and seek the verbal opinions of other people.

The notion of 'thinking style' is basically a recognition, or an acknowledgment that people think and understand in different ways. Different people develop their sensory capabilities to different degrees. Some people are naturally very visual. Some people have a very difficult time forming visual images, or thinking visually at all. Some people are more verbal, and can speak and articulate experiences very easily, while other people struggle with words. Words confuse them. Some people are very feeling-oriented, and learn or understand something through action. A leader needs to address the fact that people have different strengths.

A major part of communication strategy is directed not only at what messages collaborators should receive, but in determining which channel of communication will be most effective for delivering those messages and the meta messages necessary for them to be interpreted appropriately.

The representational channel an individual uses to present information, such as desired future events and potential consequences, is not simply a trivial detail. For example, some people run into problems accomplishing tasks because they have great visions but no comprehension of the feeling of effort that it might take to accomplish the vision, or no realization of the logical sequence of activities leading to the goal.

Take a moment and examine the way you use these different representational channels internally and externally while you are leading others. For example, when you are setting goals, are the goals represented visually? Are they represented as actions, physically? Are they represented verbally? Perhaps they are represented simply as a kind of feeling.

Similarly, you might check whether the evidence you are utilizing to confirm whether you are accomplishing your goals is verbal, visual, emotional or physical.

When you present goals and ideas to people do you tend to be primarily verbal? Or do you also use pictures and imagery, or physically act out ideas by giving 'micro demonstrations'? Perhaps you have a clear preference for one of these representational channels.

It is dangerous to automatically assume that others have the same thinking style as our own. Sometimes a person is not used to visualizing, even though people are talking about things that require the ability to remember or fantasize visually. At other times a person might tend to focus too much on a particular image that has become imprinted in his or her mind. It stands out because it's unique or it's the only one that person has been exposed to. In challenging or stressful situations, people often revert to their most familiar representational channel.

We often make assumptions that others have the same cognitive capabilities that we do. But most often this is not the case. In communicating with others, matching their channel of representation is an important method of establishing rapport and insuring that they will understand your communication.

Understanding can be enhanced by either utilizing people's strengths or strengthening their weaknesses. If somebody typically does not use visualization, encouraging them to think in terms of pictures could be very useful for them. If somebody is good at visualizing, emphasizing and enriching the use of that capability can also help to increase his or her ability to understand and perform in certain situations.

It is also possible to use several types of representations or representational channels when leading. For example, goals on a task level might be represented in terms of a picture or image of the desired result, but goals on a relational level might be represented verbally or emotionally. Certain ideas or concepts may be represented in terms of multiple senses such as feelings and imagery.

As an analogy, consider for a moment which of the following houses would appeal to you the most:

The first house is quite picturesque. It has a very quaint look to it. You can see that a major focus has been put on the colorful patio and garden area. It has a lot of window space so that you can enjoy the view. It is clearly a good buy.

The second house is very soundly constructed and well situated. It is in such a quiet area that all you hear when you walk outside are the sounds of the birds singing. Its storybook interior speaks of so much character that you'll probably find yourself asking yourself how you could ever pass it by.

The third house is not only solidly constructed, it has a very special feeling to it as well. It's not often that you come in contact with a place that touches you in so many ways because of its wide range of special features. It is spacious enough that you really feel like you can move around freely and yet cozy enough that you won't wear yourself out taking care of it.

Which one would you choose?

Actually, these are all descriptions of the same house! The only difference is that each description was written to appeal to a different sense. If you chose the first house you are probably more visually (sight) oriented. If you chose house number two you are most likely more auditorally (sound) oriented. If you chose the third, you probably value your feelings more than your other senses.

Presenting a new vision or goal is a bit like presenting a house. People will have different styles of perceiving and understanding it. Pacing people's behaviors and thinking styles is a communication skill that will help collaborators to comprehend and commit to that goal or vision.

In summary, representational channels may be used to facilitate effective communication in a number of ways:

1) Emphasizing the representational channel that is most appropriate or best suited to the type of task.

2) Matching the channel that is most frequently used and valued by the receiver(s) (appealing to a strength).

3) Using a channel that is not frequently used to stimulate new ways of thinking or perceiving (strengthening a weakness).

Basic Perceptual Positions in Communication and Relationships

To be a more effective 'sender' it is important to know something about your intended receiver(s). Developing better observational skills for non-verbal cues, pacing and mirroring physiology and language patterns, as well as gaining more flexibility in the use of different representational channels and thinking styles are all ways of accomplishing this goal.

Another way to understand people better when you are communicating with them is to 'put yourself in their shoes'. This serves to shift your "perceptual position" with respect to an interaction. In my study of effective leaders, many of them mentioned that it was important for a leader to understand the characteristics of his or her collaborators by somehow entering their viewpoint or "feeling space."

Certainly, our perceptions of situations and experiences are greatly influenced by the point of view or perspective from which we consider them. In addition to being in the shoes of another person, there are several basic "perceptual positions" from which an interaction may be viewed. Perceptual positions refer to the fundamental points of view one can take concerning the relationship between oneself and another person:

1st Position: Associated in your own point of view, beliefs and assumptions, seeing the external world through your own eyes – an *"I"* position.

2nd Position: Associated in another person's point of view, beliefs and assumptions, seeing the external world through his or her eyes – a *"you"* position.

3rd Position: Associated in a point of view outside of the relationship between yourself and the other person – a *"they"* position.

4th Position: Associated in the perspective of the whole system – a *"we"* position. This is what one leader described as a "thinking vision of the system."

As the descriptions above indicate, perceptual positions are characterized and expressed by key words – "I," "you," "they," and "we." In a way, these key words are a type of meta message that can help you to recognize and direct the perceptual positions people are assuming during a particular interaction. For instance, someone who frequently uses the word "I" is more likely to be speaking from his or her point of view than a person who is using the word "we" when talking about ideas or suggestions. A person who is stuck in one perspective can be paced and lead to shift perceptual positions through the subtle use of such language cues.

For example, let's say a member of a project team is being overly critical of an idea or plan and says something like, "*I* don't think this will ever work", indicating a strong 'first position' reaction. The leader could pace and lead the individual to a more 'systemic' position by saying, "I understand you have some big concerns about this plan. How do you think *we* can approach it in a way that will work?"

To guide the person to an observer position, the leader could suggest, "Imagine you were a consultant for this team. What ways would you suggest for *them* to work together more effectively?" To encourage the critical individual to go to 'second position' the leader could say, "Put yourself in my shoes (or one of the other team members) for a moment. What reactions do you think I would have to *your* concern?"

Certainly, one of the most important communication and relational skills a leader can develop for himself or herself is the ability to switch points of view and take multiple perspectives of a situation or experience. Try taking the different perceptual positions with respect to a leadership situation by practicing the following steps.

1. Think about a challenging situation you have been in, or are expecting to be in, involving a particular collaborator.

2. Put yourself fully into 1st position by imagining that your collaborator is here right now and that you are looking at him or her through your own eyes.

3. Now imagine you are "in the shoes" of your collaborator looking at your self through his or her eyes. Assume the perspective, beliefs and assumptions of the collaborator as if you were that person for a moment.

4. Now view the relationship between yourself and your collaborator as if you were an observer watching a video of some other leader interacting with a collaborator.

5. As a final experiment, take the perspective of the whole system and consider what would be in the best interest of the system.

Notice how taking the different perceptual positions changes your experience of the interaction.

What new awareness did you get about yourself, your collaborator or the situation?

The Skill of Meta Communication

Another key communication skill for effective leadership relates to the process of "meta communication". *Meta communication* is 'communication about communication'. For instance, a meta communication is often a verbal statement that sets a framework around a communication situation in the form of rules, guidelines and expectations. It essentially involves setting the frame for an interaction. A leader 'meta communicates' about a situation in order to set up appropriate expectations and presuppositions in an individual or a group. Before a leader initiates a meeting or an interaction, for example, he or she may decide to set certain guidelines, rules of interaction, directions for interpretation, etc.

It is important to distinguish meta communication from 'meta messages'. Meta communication is a more macro level process than sending a meta message. A meta message is a message about another specific message. It operates as a kind of non-verbal subtext that emphasizes certain aspects of a message. As I pointed out earlier, if a person says, "YOU weren't respecting the rules," emphasizing the "You" with voice inflection, it marks the communication as directed toward the 'who'. Saying, "You weren't respecting the RULES," shifts the emphasis of the message to the 'what'.

Meta communication, on the other hand, would be saying something like, "Let's talk about what the rules are and why we have them." "What are the goals and purposes of the rules?" In other words, meta communication would involve initiating a discussion *about* the rules. Meta communication might be saying something like, "It's important for us to respect this", or "The rules help us to avoid that."

The statement, "Looking back on your comment from the company's point of view, you'd have to admit that..." is a meta communication that is telling the listener what perceptual position ('company's point of view') and representational channel ('looking', 'view') that could be essential for sharing the intended meaning of the message, "You weren't respecting the rules." Thus, meta communication addresses the framework surrounding the rest of the communication.

In my study of the communication patterns of effective leaders, I observed that almost half of the leaders' communication was actually meta communication. Effective leaders were constantly saying things like, "I'm going to be talking about this..." "This is how I want you to think about it." "Focus here..." "Have these types of expectations.." It is as if they were setting up all of the elements necessary to interpret their communication accurately before they finally made the one essential point. Because the interpretation and understanding of that one point is so significant, they needed to cover all the 'perceptual space' around it so there was no ambiguity.

Meta communication is often necessary in order to establish or clarify the context of a communication. When a leader enters into an unfamiliar culture, for instance, he or she may spend quite a bit of time meta communicating before actually beginning a meeting or interaction. This can help to set the framework for people to accurately interpret both verbal and non-verbal messages. If the leader doesn't provide any contextual information, he or she can only hope that people will share a similar enough awareness and understanding to be able to interpret messages appropriately.

Meta communication also involves 'talking about' what is happening during a communication interaction in order to make conscious or acknowledge some significant aspect of the interaction. Therefore, if a leader feels that there is something going on in a group that seems ambiguous, he or she might choose to go back and clarify some of the issues or assumptions by meta communicating about the situation.

The amount of meta communication one uses is a strategic choice. For example, when a leader goes into a new situation, he or she might spend more time meta communicating than if it was a more familiar context.

Practicing Effective Communication Skills

The following exercise will help you to explore how the distinctions, principles and skills that have been outlined in this chapter relate to the personal experience of leadership. Its purpose is to underline some principles of effective leadership and to make you aware of some aspects of your own leadership skills and style through a concrete reference experience.

There are two roles in the exercise; a 'leader' and a 'group'. The 'leader' is to make a presentation to the group about a 'vision' that the leader has. The group members are to listen to the presentation, observe the leader and notice if there are patterns and consistencies of language and behavior relating to the leaders's skills and style.

Part I – Preparing the 'Intended' Message

Instructions for the 'Leader'

Your task is to make a short presentation and lead a discussion about a 'vision' that you have. (The presentation and discussion should take no longer than 10-15 minutes.) Refer to one of the vision statements you created in Chapter 2 or 3.

Before interacting with the group, prepare your 'intended' message and communication strategy. Imagine putting yourself into the shoes of the group members and anticipate how they might respond to the vision you are presenting. Consider which representational channel or channels would be the most effective means to convey the information (i.e., verbal, visual, written, enacted, etc.). Also, define the set of intended 'meta messages' you would like to communicate in relation to your vision including:

- Your internal state.
- The type of relationship you want to have with the group (complementary, symmetrical, reciprocal).
- The desired internal state for the group members.
- The type of context for your interaction (i.e., teaching, brainstorming, motivational, etc.).

Determine which communication channels (voice inflection, gestures, body posture, 'psychogeography', etc.) you will use to communicate your desired meta messages. Also, determine which issues might be most important to 'meta communicate' about prior to or during the interaction.

Before interacting with the group, it is also a good idea to go through the process for creating an 'aligned state', described in Chapter 2.

Part II – Delivering the Message

Instructions for the 'Leader'

Make your presentation and conduct a brief discussion about your vision. While you are engaged in the interaction, see if you can begin to develop a 'meta cognition' (an introspective awareness) of your own processes and strategies – especially in terms of how you use language and representational channels. Try to experience the impact of language and the different representational channels on the group. In the back of your mind, start paying attention to what type of skills you utilize. How do you communicate your vision? What satisfies you that you've presented 'enough'?

Observe the group and notice what kinds of non-verbal cues you are aware of. How do you respond to those cues as feedback while managing your interaction with the group? How do you maintain your own state and influence the state of the group members?

Instructions for the 'Group'

While the 'leader' is making the presentation, group members are to observe for key verbal and behavioral patterns demonstrated by the leader. The group should pay particular attention to how the 'leader' (a) communicates information and (b) interacts with the group members.

Group members should be aware that there is a difference between *observation* and *interpretation*. Observations are descriptions of actual behaviors, not inferences or projections about what those behaviors might mean.

Group members are to focus on what is 'relevant' (i.e., what repeats, changes the most, or is the most exaggerated) in the language and physical behavior of the 'leader'. The group should pay particular attention to key non-verbal cues such as body posture, facial expression, voice tone, and gestures.

Part III – Determining the 'Received' Message

After the 'leader' has finished, each group member is to define the message and meta messages he or she has 'received'.

Each group member is to begin by making some notes or writing a short description of the 'content' of the presentation and discussion – i.e., what is the leader's vision? Each person should do this individually, without any direct interaction with other group members.

Next, each group member is to record what he or she has received in relation to the 'leader's' meta messages by answering the following questions:

- What state was the leader in?

- What type of relationship did the leader want to have with you (the group) - complementary, symmetrical, reciprocal?

- What kind of state did the leader want you (the group) to be in?

- What was the type of context of the interaction (i.e., teaching, brainstorming, motivational, etc.)?

Part IV – Reflecting on the Process

The final stage of this exercise involves reflecting on the types of communication skills involved in the interaction.

First, compare the 'intended' and 'received' messages and meta messages. Note what aspects of the leader's intended messages and meta messages he or she was successful in conveying. Discuss which elements of the communication matrix were involved in that success (i.e., representational channels, non-verbal cues, 'psychogeography', meta communication, etc.).

Also note where there were discrepancies between the intended and received message and meta messages. Try to identify which non-verbal cues, interpretations and assumptions account for those discrepancies. As a group, explore the ways in which the message or meta messages could have been more successfully communicated. This can be done by role playing alternative scenarios and assessing their viability and effectiveness.

Discuss how the 'leader' used non-verbal communication and 'meta messages' in the form of gestures, voice tone and 'psychogeography'. Which representational channels did he or she use effectively? In what ways did the leader naturally 'pace and lead' people? Which perspectives and perceptual position language did he or she emphasize? At which level was the presentation and discussion focused (what, how, why, who, etc.)? What cues did the leader use as feedback from the group? What they said? How they looked? What they did?

Remember, this is a general exploration; a discovery exercise. Its purpose is to practice some of the communication skills we have explored in this chapter. The attitude to take towards this kind of exercise is that of being open to discover or explore; of being curious about learning something about your own process and improving as a leader and a communicator. That's how you'll get the most out of it.

Some other questions to consider include:

- What aspects of your verbal and non-verbal behavior are in your awareness? What are some of the 'unconscious competences' you discovered?

- How was your leadership 'style' and skill similar to or different from other group members?

- Did you encounter any unexpected difficulties or challenges? How did you respond to them?

- Did any beliefs come up or play a part in this experience?

- How similar were the communication and relational skills you used in this circumstance to what you might do in a typical leadership situation?

- What did you learn from this process?

It is important to keep in mind that different people have different styles and strategies, even for a simple task. Some of these differences relate to the type of goals one sets. A more physical strategy might be more effective than a more verbal or visual approach for some types of situations.

Most of you will probably notice the distinction between your own conscious versus unconscious competences. You will probably not be aware of everything you are doing while you are doing it. Many of you may also discover that there are a number of simultaneous processes to keep track of while leading the interaction. Even in a very simple situation there are combinations of different communication skills and leadership styles.

Chapter 7

Leadership Styles

Overview of Chapter 7

- Influence of Different Leadership Styles
- Situational Leadership
- Transformational Leadership
- Leadership Style Assessment Sheet
- Levels of Change and Leadership Styles
- Exploring and Expanding Leadership Style

Influence of Different Leadership Styles

As we have established, a leader is an individual who uses his or her influence to 'lead' a group of collaborators to reach desired goals within a particular system. In this respect, a leader serves as both:

1) a facilitator of the relationship and

2) the focal point of the task.

To effectively accomplish both functions, it is important for leaders to understand and develop flexibility in their own leadership styles. One principle of leadership and communication is that certain types of leadership styles and communication strategies might be effective in certain contexts but may be less effective in others.

One important factor influencing a leader's choice of communication strategy and leadership style relates to the culture of his or her collaborators. Culture is often embodied in presuppositions and rules. Rules establish constraints and reflect beliefs and values. It is important for a leader to identify and address constraints, beliefs and values and to consider what is presupposed by his or her own style as well as the styles of others.

Another factor influencing a leader's communication strategy and leadership style is the level of change required by the goals or objectives to be reached. For instance, issues relating to the level of values and ethics might be handled differently than issues at the level of behaviors and procedures. While clear and direct communication may be the most effective approach for changes in behaviors or procedures, values are often best communicated indirectly – direct statements of values and ethics may be perceived as 'preaching'. In this sense, "actions will speak louder than words." Thus, values are often communicated more effectively in terms of meta messages, relationships and interactions not directly related to a particular task. Similarly, evidences of change in values and ethics are also more indirect indicators such as change in the quality of people's relationships with others and activities that are analogous, rather than directly related to the task.

Leaders will have different degrees of conscious awareness of behavioral cues, meta messages, group dynamics, etc. This often effects the style and strategy they use to lead a group. People often have many unconscious competences of which they are not aware.

Also, a leader's beliefs and assumptions influence the way that he or she manages a group or a situation. A person's beliefs and assumptions will often determine what he or she sorts for as evidence in various stages of a project or interaction and how he or she interprets behavioral cues, meta messages, group dynamics, etc.

Obviously, there is no one right way to lead an individual or group. Different styles encourage different dynamics between members of a system. Sometimes collaborators have to become familiar with a particular leadership style in order for it to become effective for them.

The most important reason for learning about different leadership styles is to increase your success in a wider variety of situations. This is accomplished through developing the flexibility to adapt your style more effectively to the needs of a particular situation or context.

Situational Leadership

One of the most prevalent and popular models of 'leadership style' is that of *situational leadership* developed by Blanchard and Hersey. Situational leadership is clearly what Nicholls had in mind in his definition of 'micro leadership', which, he maintained, *"focuses on the choice of leadership **style** to create an efficient working atmosphere and obtain willing cooperation in getting the job done by adjusting one's style on the twin dimensions of task and relationship behavior. Choice of leadership style depends on the particular subordinates and the job/task being done, it is, thus, situational and contingent...the leader directs people in organizations in the accomplishment of a specific job or task. If the leadership style is correctly attuned, people perform willingly in an efficient working atmosphere."*

According to Hersey (1984) the Situational Leadership model, *"provides a framework from which to diagnose different situations and prescribes which leader behaviors will have the highest probability of success...Situational Leadership is based on an interplay among (1) amounts of task behavior a leader provides; (2) the amount of relationship behavior a leader provides; and (3) the readiness level that followers demonstrate in performing a specific task or activity...When attempting to influence others, your job is to (1) diagnose the readiness level of the follower for a specific task; and (2) provide the appropriate leadership style for that situation."*

(1) Task behavior is defined as: *"the extent to which the leader engages in spelling out the duties and responsibilities of an individual or group. The behaviors include telling people what to do, how to do it, when to do it, where to do it and who's to do it."*

(2) Relationship behavior is defined as: *"the extent to which the leader engages in two-way or multi-way communication if there is more than one person. The behaviors include listening, encouraging, facilitating, providing clarification, and giving socioemotional support."*

(3) Readiness is defined as: *"the extent to which a follower has the ability and willingness to accomplish a specific task."* Where: *"ability is the knowledge, experience, and skill that an individual or group brings to a particular task or activity. Willingness has to do with confidence, commitment, and motivation to accomplish a specific task or activity."*

Situational leadership 'styles' are divided into four categories that are 'attuned' to four levels of 'readiness'.

1. Style 1 (S1) - For collaborators who lack both ability and willingness.
   This leadership style is characterized by above average amounts of task behavior and below average amounts of relationship behavior. Leader Style 1 is directive. It consists of telling the individual or group what to do, when, where, how and with whom to do it. Style one is typified by one-way communication in which the leader directs the followers toward accomplishing tasks and reaching goals.

2. Style 2 (S2) - For collaborators who have some ability and some willingness.
   This leadership style is characterized by above average amounts of both task and relationship behavior. Leader Style 2 still provides guidance. The leader's actions and statements exhibit moderate to high amounts of task

behavior. At the same time the leader provides explanations and opportunities for clarification.

3. Style 3 (S3) - For collaborators who are capable but unwilling.

   This leadership style is characterized by above average amounts of relationship behavior and below average amounts of task behavior. Style 3 is characterized by leader behavior that provides encouragement, promotes discussion, and asks for contributions from the followers.

4. Style 4 (S4) - For collaborators who are both able and willing.

   This leadership style is characterized by below average amounts of both task behavior and relationship behavior. Style 4 leader behavior provides little direction, and low amounts of two-way communication and supportive behavior.

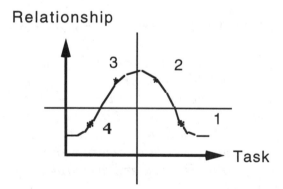

Situational Leadership Styles

Hersey defines 'leadership style' as: *"the patterns of behavior (words and actions) of the leader* **as perceived by others.** *Leadership style is always defined in terms of how the leader appears in the eyes of the beholder. It's not how people see* *themselves that matters, but how they come across to others they're attempting to influence."*

According to this definition, 'style' is primarily an issue of relationship. Leadership style is less determined by the task one is managing than the type of relationship and 'atmosphere' with collaborators the leader is attempting to create. Most importantly it is determined in regard to the collaborators' subjective response to the leader.

In contrast to this definition of leadership style, however, in the model of situational leadership the leader selects types of behavior based upon his or her *own* perception of the collaborator's readiness in regard to an external task. The situational leadership model is (as the name implies) about responding to a 'situation' as perceived by the leader, not about influencing the perceptions of collaborators. Thus, it does not overtly address issues of leadership style that involve such things as the collaborator's personality, thinking style, values, perception of the context, etc. In a way, situational leadership seems to be more a model of 'management' than of leadership.

Transformational Leadership

Bass (1985) identifies two basic classes of leadership – 'transactional' and 'transformational'. Transactional leaders tend to be primarily action oriented, whereas transformational leaders tend to use a higher degree of vision. Some leadership involves the development of primarily 'transactional' skills, while others require 'transformational' processes.

Transformational leadership is defined along the dimensions of 'vision' and 'action' as opposed to 'task and 'relationship'. 'Vision' has to do with creating images of future goals. 'Action' has to do with the execution of immediate behaviors. The general idea is that *"vision without action is just a dream; and action without vision is meaningless and boring."*

Bass breaks these down further into several leadership styles associated with the classes of leadership. These styles are defined by the following characteristics:

Non-Leadership

Laissez-Faire: Avoids decisions, withdraws when needed, uninvolved and takes no stand.

Transactional Leadership

- **Management By Exception:** Intervention only when collaborators deviate from expectations. As long as things are going according to expectation, he or she does not try to change anything. Gives negative feedback when there is a failure to meet standards.

- **Contingent Reward:** Contracts an exchange of reward for effort. Tells collaborators what to do if they want to be rewarded. Assures collaborators that they can get what they want in exchange for effort. Gives special commendations and promotions for good work.

Transformational Leadership

- **Management by Objective:** Provides collaborators with clear representations of the desired goals and evidences to know when the goals have been achieved. Encourages collaborators to use their own capabilities and resources. *

- **Intellectual Stimulation:** Leader's ideas compel collaborators to rethink some of their own ideas. Old problems are thought of in new ways. Stresses intelligence, rationality and careful problem solving.

- **Inspirational:** Operates as a kind of "cheerleader" motivating and encouraging collaborators to do their best or to give a little extra. Emphasizes values, empowering beliefs in future possibilities.

- **Individualized Consideration:** Gives personalized attention to neglected members, treats each collaborator individually, coaches and advises.

- **Charismatic** (Idealized Influence): Has a sense of vision, mission, and gives collaborators a sense of purpose. Is a model collaborators want to follow. Gains respect and trust.

As a simple (and somewhat metaphorical) illustration of what these different styles might look like in a 'micro leadership' situation, let's return to the couple in front of the television set that we visited as an example in the previous chapter. Let's say that the wife has become dissatisfied with the arrangement of the furniture in their living room (sofa, TV, etc.) and would like to change their locations. This would put her in the role of 'leader' and her husband in the role of 'collaborator'.

---

* 'Management by objective' is not actually a style defined or assessed by Bass. I have included it, however, because I think it is a common and important leadership style, and it does fit into the system of styles proposed by the Bass model.

If the wife were to assume a *laissez-faire* style of leadership, she might simply say to her husband, "Are you satisfied with the way the furniture is arranged in this room?" She would hope her husband would get the message that she wanted something changed, but would take no stand of her own regarding decisions about the placement of the furniture.

If the wife decided to become more 'transactional' she would actually ask her husband directly if he would rearrange the furniture. Were she to take on the style of *management by exception*, however, she would offer no direct guidance about where exactly to place it. After he moved the sofa somewhere, she might look it over and say, "No, I don't like it there. Move it somewhere else." "No, I don't like it there either. Why don't you try another location?" This type of interaction would go on until, hopefully, the husband stumbled upon an acceptable location.

If she were to operate more from a style of *contingent reward*, she would be more directive. She might say, "No, if you put the sofa there, it will be too close to the window and I'll complain about the cold all the time. If you move it another couple of feet to the left, it would still get light from the window and we would have a good angle with respect to the television." "That's a little better. Thanks, you're doing a good job. I've got your favorite dish ready for supper when you're finished. Now about the lamp, I think it would be better..."

If the wife were to approach the task from the more 'transformational' style of *management by objective*, she would first lay out a very clear representation of her desired state for the furniture. She might draw a picture showing the exact locations in the room that she would like to have the various pieces of furniture placed. She might comment to her husband about some of her reasoning and criteria, and express her appreciation for her husband's ability to move such bulky furniture as well as his willingness to help.

Were the wife to take on the style of *intellectual stimulation*, she might first sit with her husband and discuss with him the placement of the furniture. She might point out some of the problems she has experienced with the current arrangement of the furniture and ask him what ideas he had about possible solutions to those problems. She might describe some of her own ideas about possible arrangements and ask him for his responses and input, periodically asking, "What do you think?" After considering his responses she would ask questions clarifying his reasoning for certain suggestions and ideas.

If the wife were to become more *inspirational* in her style, she might talk about how "wonderful" and "exciting" it would be to have a new arrangement for the furniture in the room. She might comment on how much it would enhance their enjoyment of the room and how much easier it would make things for them. She might also talk about how pleased her husband had been with some of the past projects he had been involved with that improved the house, and point out how such a small amount of effort can make such a big difference.

To assume the style of *individualized consideration*, the wife might sit with her husband and focus on what he liked, disliked and wanted most from that particular room and the arrangement of the furniture. She might ask, "What would *you* like to get out of this project?" She would stress how important his feelings and values were, giving him time to consider each question fully. She would also attempt to put herself in his shoes and ask if there was anything that might make the job of rearranging the furniture easier or more efficient.

Were the wife to become *charismatic* in her style, she might discuss her long term vision for her relationship with her husband and their life together. She would talk about their home, and how each room was an important reflection of that vision. She might mention that her husband's assistance with even the details of the arrangement of furniture in their home was an important part of their relationship, and that it gave her concrete feedback about his commitment to their marriage and of the vision they shared of their future together.

Obviously, the different styles involve more or less emphasis on aspects of 'task' versus 'relationship', and on 'vision' versus 'action'. They also involve assumptions about the quality of relationship between the 'leader' and 'collaborator(s)' as well as their respective skills and capabilities.

According to the model, the more transformational factors the collaborator perceives in the leader, the more effective the leader is, regardless of the specific situation. The leader's task is to change his or her behavior in a way that increases the amount of transformational qualities perceived by collaborators.

While this model undoubtedly has many merits, there are some potential draw backs. For instance, the model does not provide a system of behavioral micro skills or cognitive strategies to direct the leader as to how specifically to change his or her behavior in order to influence his or her collaborators' perceptions. Clearly, such micro skills would involve the ability to send certain meta messages as well as messages – otherwise the style will appear 'forced' or 'fake'.

Perhaps more importantly, the model does not necessarily take into account individual differences between situations and types of tasks, goals and collaborators that might make one of the styles (even the transactional styles) more appropriate for some contexts than it would for others.

For instance, as a father of two young children, I find that there is often value in some of the transactional leadership styles in effectively managing the behavior of my children. If the two of them are playing together happily, there is less need for explicit 'leadership' on my part. My involvement may even interfere with their own creativity and imagination. So, I assume a style of *management by exception*. As long as there is no crying or fighting, I don't intervene. Even when there is, I might first see if they can work out the problem on their own.

When it is time for the children to clean their rooms or get their pajamas on, however, I must shift to a style involving more *management by objective* and *contingent reward* (perhaps even some *inspiration* on occasion). In doing a project or homework for school, *intellectual stimulation* is more appropriate. And if there has been an emotional incident resulting in tears, a healthy dose of *individualized consideration* is in order.

In fact, it seems to me that the different leadership styles form a natural sequence. The leader begins by presenting the vision, then shifts to individualized consideration in order to better understand the beliefs and values of collaborators. Inspiration involves connecting those beliefs and values to the vision. Intellectual stimulation then helps people to consider ways to manifest the vision. Afterwards, specific objectives may be set and a system of rewards worked out. If these steps have been accomplished effectively, leadership shifts to the collaborators and the leader is able to operate from management by exception.

Assessing Leadership Styles

It seems evident that different people will have their own natural leadership style and proclivities, which will be more or less effective based on the culture, context, type of collaborators and desired outcomes. One aspect of an effective communication strategy is for the leader to develop a better sense of his or her own leadership style and enrich it in order to be effective in a wider variety of situations.

In assessing leadership styles it is important to note that Bass determines these styles based on the subjective opinions of collaborators, rather than on the leaders' self evaluation. Therefore, assessing one's own leadership style requires the ability to take 'second position' with collaborators.

The *Leadership Assessment Sheet* on the following pages provides an instrument for assessing one's leadership style. To fill it in, first identify a particular collaborator and a common leadership situation that you would like to explore. To rate your style, review your behavior in the situation from either the perspective of an observer or from the perceptual position of your collaborator.

Another way to use the sheet would be to fill it out yourself, using your own subjective perception of your style. Then have your collaborator fill it out, and compare your ratings.

Leadership Style Assessment Sheet

Rate the leader's mix of styles using the following scale:
4 = frequently, if not always, 3 = fairly often, 2 = sometimes,
1 = hardly ever, 0 = never.

- **Management By Exception:** *Intervention only when collaborators deviate from expectations. As long as things are going according to expectations, he or she does not try to change anything. Gives negative feedback when there is a failure to meet standards.*

| 0 | 1 | 2 | 3 | 4 |

- **Contingent Reward:** *Contracts exchange of reward for effort. Tells collaborators what to do if they want to be rewarded. Assures collaborators that they can get what they want in exchange for their effort. Gives special commendations and promotions for good work.*

| 0 | 1 | 2 | 3 | 4 |

- **Management by Objective:** *Provides collaborators with clear representations of the desired goals and evidences to know when the goals have been achieved. Encourages collaborators to use their own capabilities and resources.*

| 0 | 1 | 2 | 3 | 4 |

- **Intellectual Stimulation:** *Leader's ideas compel collaborators to rethink some of their own ideas. Old problems are thought of in new ways. Stresses intelligence, rationality and careful problem solving.*

- **Inspirational:** *Operates as a kind of "cheerleader" motivating and encouraging collaborators to do their best or give a little extra. Emphasizes values, empowering beliefs in future possibilities.*

- **Individualized Consideration:** *Gives personalized attention to neglected members, treats each collaborator individually, coaches and advises.*

- **Charismatic:** *Has a sense of vision and mission, and gives collaborators a sense of purpose. Is a model collaborators want to follow. Gains respect and trust.*

Assessment of Leadership Styles of 'World-Class' Level Leaders

Bass and Avolio (1987) used a similar type of assessment process to examine how 'world class' leaders differed with respect to these various leadership factors using biographical accounts. The scores of some well-known leaders are listed below [4 = frequently, if not always, 3 = fairly often, 2 = sometimes, 1 = hardly ever, 0 = never].

	Charismatic	Individualized Consideration	Intellectual Stimulation	Contingent Reward	Management by Exception
Martin Luther King	3.9	2.5	3.4	2.4	1.9
Mahatma Gandhi	3.8	3.3	3.5	2.1	1.5
John F. Kennedy	3.6	3.1	3.4	2.0	1.9
Abraham Lincoln	2.9	2.6	2.9	1.9	2.0
Adolph Hitler	3.4	1.0	2.0	1.9	3.1
Joseph Stalin	2.7	2.1	2.4	1.9	2.3

Considering these various individuals and their styles can help to give you a better idea of the different leadership styles and their impact.

Leadership Styles and Managing Beliefs

If you reflect on the various belief issues outlined in Chapter 5, it will probably be clear that different leadership styles are more suited to address different belief issues. For instance, if there is doubt about the desirability of the goal or outcome, a style emphasizing inspiration or individualized consideration would be more effective than management by objective. If there is doubt relating to the appropriateness or possibility of the path, intellectual stimulation would be more helpful. Clarity issues would be most effectively addressed through management by objective and contingent reward. Concerns about capability, responsibility and worthiness would require a combination of individualized consideration, inspiration and intellectual stimulation. All belief issues, however, are most effectively managed when embedded in the larger context of the vision.

Levels of Change and Leadership Styles

Leadership is needed in situations requiring influence. Styles of leadership can be related to the level of change that the leader is attempting to influence. Different styles of leadership are needed when influence is focused upon different levels of change. In the path of achieving a desired state, a leader directs his or her influence toward different levels of learning and experience. He or she thus might use several leadership styles depending on the goals and phase of the task or project, as well as the degree of proactivity or reactivity required from the leader.

For instance, in some activities and situations, the leader may want collaborators to be highly proactive so they can act based on their own skills and competence. In such cases the leader's style may shift to one of 'management by exception'. That is, the leader primarily directs his or her influence toward the context or environment surrounding and supporting the activity and only intervenes if collaborators experience a problem or difficulty.

Other situations and activities may require more proactive input and supervision from the leader. In such cases the leader may assume a style of 'intellectual stimulation'. For leadership tasks that require the establishment or change of beliefs and values, it may be more effective for the leader to shift to a style involving individualized consideration, creating a space for individuals to discuss their personal opinions, motivation and beliefs.

Thus, the communication strategy of the leader will require that the leader adapt his or her leadership style appropriately to the level of influence and change required by the context or task:

- When influence is directed towards the *environment* (where/when), the leader intervenes only if something is going wrong or deviating from the 'status quo' – *'laissez-faire' and management by exception.*

- When influence is directed toward specific changes of *behavior* (what), the leader sets up a clear system of *contingent rewards* – positive or negative reinforcement based on collaborators' actions.

- Influence at the level of *capability* (how) is accomplished by providing clear objectives and stimulating intellectual processes – *management by objective and intellectual stimulation.*

- Leadership styles directed toward influencing *beliefs and values* (why) involve the consideration of individual motivations and values as well as the attempt to inspire group members – *individualized consideration* and *inspirational.*

- Influence at the level of *identity* (who) often comes through the identification of a shared vision or a figure representing a common 'role model' – *charismatic.*

Level of Influence	Outcome	Leadership Style(s)
Spiritual	*Vision*	Visionary
Identity	*Mission*	Charismatic
Beliefs	*Permission*	Individual Consideration
	Motivation	Inspirational
Capabilities	*Perception*	Intellectual Stimulation
	Direction	Management by Objective
Behavior	*Action*	Contingent Reward
Environment	*Reaction*	Management by Exception

Exercise - Exploring and Expanding Leadership Style

According to the *Law of Requisite Variety* in systems theory, flexibility is required in order to consistently reach the same goals because situations and systems change. Therefore, the more flexible a person is in his or her map and leadership style, the more effective leader that person will be.

The purpose of the following exercise is to provide you with an opportunity to learn more about your own natural leadership style and to enrich your own repertoire of leadership styles. It is also an opportunity for you to explore other styles of leading group interactions and experience the impact and effectiveness of different leadership styles.

Preparing Your State

The subtleties of the messages and meta messages associated with various leadership styles are not easy to produce consciously or analytically. They flow naturally, however, from your state. A good way to prepare for this exercise is to lay out seven spaces for the various leadership styles. For each style, identify a personal reference experience for a time when you were able to effectively express that style. Stand in the space associated with each style, and notice the types of movements, voice tone and internal state related to the experience. As a final step, align all of the styles together within the context of your vision (similar to the Level Alignment processdescribed in Chapter 2).

The basic steps in the exercise are:

1. Form small groups.

2. One group member is to be the 'leader' and identify a goal, type of collaborators and a context.

3. The 'leader' determines:

   a) The level of focus of the goal (behavior, capability, beliefs, etc.).

   b) The degree of vision versus action required to reach the goal.

   c) The amount of focus upon task versus relationship required by the goal.

   d) Any potential belief issues related to the goal.

4. The 'leader' then selects his or her 'intended' mix of leadership styles (using the 'Leadership Style Assessment Sheet' provided earlier). The leader should plan an appropriate communication strategy (i.e., messages, meta messages, state and status) that will support the chosen mix of leadership styles. The leader is to prepare to enact his or her mix of styles by adjusting his or her internal state to bring that style into the foreground.

5. The rest of the group divides into role players and observers. The role players interact with the 'leader' according to the type of collaborators and context that the leader has defined. During the interaction, the 'leader' is to attempt to enact his or her chosen mix of styles.

6. After the role play, the individual group members (both role players and observers) rate the leader's mix of styles (using the *Leadership Style Assessment Sheet*). If there are discrepancies in the leader's intended mix of styles and the mix of styles perceived by the group, discuss the reasons for those differences in terms of the behavioral cues of the leader (messages, meta messages, physiology, etc.).

7. The group should also reflect upon the effectiveness of the leader's interaction and mix of leadership styles. (Refer to the questions provided for the *Effective Communication* exercise at the end of Chapter 6.) Suggested variations and alternatives may be discussed and role played.

Chapter 8

The Parable of the Porpoise

Overview of Chapter 8

- A New Paradigm for Learning and Leadership
- The Parable of the Porpoise
- Levels of Learning
- Context and Presuppositions
- Culture and 'Learning II'
- Implications of the Parable of the Porpoise for Leadership
- Applying the Parable of the Porpoise

A New Paradigm for Learning and Leadership

Methods for managing change and learning are based on fundamental assumptions about behavior. The way one approaches a task or situation is based upon underlying presuppositions and assumptions which are often outside of one's awareness. These assumptions and presuppositions form what is called a 'paradigm'.

As an example, most theories of learning, motivation and management are centered around the paradigm of the *'reflex arc'*. According to this paradigm, behavior is a result of a mechanical process in which we (a) take in some sensory **stimulus**, which (b) causes some **response**, which is (c) subsequently either positively or negatively **reinforced**. Much of the research designed to support this paradigm has been done with rats, pigeons and dogs.

While people may not realize it, most of the techniques of leadership and management are based upon the presuppositions of the reflex arc. Management skills often center around developing the ability to give clearer stimuli to the employee, developing specific behavioral responses and providing appropriate 'reinforcements' in terms of praise, monetary rewards, fringe benefits, etc. As modern organizations becomes more sophisticated, however, the old paradigm for learning and motivation is becoming less and less adequate as a basis to describe and prescribe the processes involved in effective leadership and management.

"Creating a world to which people want to belong" often involves a shift in pradigm. In many ways, this book has been about a paradigm shift with respect to leadership. It seems to me that the areas of management and leadership are poised to undergo a change of paradigm similar to the fundamental transition that physics underwent at the beginning of this century - moving from the Newtonian model of linear causes and effects to Einstein's more encompassing and profound relativistic model, which is based upon the relationship between the observer and the observed. In the same way, the trend in modern organizations seems to be moving away from management based on a linear chain of command (Newtonian) toward cooperative relationships (Einsteinian). The establishment of a model for leadership and management based upon context and relationship could lead to a similar type of revolution in business that Einstein's theory of relativity inspired in science.

One of the most common and powerful ways to begin a new shift in paradigm is through the process of analogy. For instance, rather than view people as rats, pigeons, dogs, or computers, the issues involved in training dolphins and porpoises seems to be a much more appropriate and respectful metaphor for understanding human behavior. Next to humans, dolphins and porpoises are considered to be the most intelligent beings. They use sophisticated communication systems with one another and their nervous system is actually more complex than that of a human being. In addition, the ratio of their brain mass to body mass is greater than that of humans.

Certainly, dolphins and porpoises are capable of much more complex behavior than rats, pigeons, dogs and even sophisticated computers. Their range of creativity and 'discretionary space' is broader. In fact, porpoise and dolphin training more frequently involves the learning of classes of behavior rather than specific behaviors like pushing a bar or running a maze. Research involving the training of dolphins - the management of their behavior - has presented some unique problems and results. Most notably (and most relevant) they are extremely sensitive to the context of their training and to their relationship with their trainer. In order to effectively train a porpoise or dolphin you must establish a relationship with it - otherwise it will ignore you, even if you are the one who feeds it.

The Parable of the Porpoise

The following story/parable outlines some potential parameters of a new paradigm for leadership and management that has been outlined in this book.

Anthropologist Gregory Bateson spent a number of years studying the communication patterns of dolphins and porpoises. He reports that, in order to supplement their scientific studies, the research center he was involved with often put on shows for live audiences using these animals - sometimes as often as three times a day. The researchers decided to demonstrate to the audience the process of how they trained a porpoise to do a trick. A porpoise would be led from a holding tank into the performing tank in front of the audience. The trainer would wait until the porpoise did some conspicuous behavior (conspicuous to humans, that is) - say, lifting its head out of the water in a certain way. The trainer would then blow a whistle and give the porpoise a fish. The trainer would then wait until the porpoise eventually repeated the behavior, blow the whistle again and give it a fish. Soon the porpoise had learned what to do to get the fish and was lifting its head quite often, providing a successful demonstration of its ability to learn.

A couple of hours later, however, the porpoise was brought back to the exhibition tank for a second show. Naturally, it began lifting its head out of the water as it did in the first show, and waited for the expected whistle and fish. The trainer, of course, didn't want the porpoise to do the same old trick, but to demonstrate to the audience how the porpoise learned a new one. After spending roughly two-thirds of the show period repeating the old trick over and over, the porpoise finally became frustrated and flipped its tail at the trainer in disgust. The trainer immediately blew the whistle and threw it a fish. The surprised and somewhat confused porpoise cautiously flipped its tail again, and again got the whistle and fish.   Soon it was merrily flipping its tail, successfully demonstrating again its ability to learn and was returned to its home tank.

At the third session, after being led to the exhibition tank, the porpoise began dutifully flipping its tail as it had learned in the previous session. However, since the trainer wanted it to learn something new, it was not rewarded. Once more, for roughly two thirds of the training session the porpoise continually repeated the head lift and tail flip with growing frustration, until finally, out of exasperation, it did something different, such as spinning itself around. The trainer immediately sounded the whistle and gave the porpoise a fish. After some time it successfully learned to spin itself for the audience and was led back to its home tank.

For fourteen straight shows the porpoise repeated this pattern - the first two thirds of the show was spent in futile repetitions of the behavior that had been reinforced in the previous shows until, seemingly by "accident", it engaged in a new piece of conspicuous behavior and was able to complete the training demonstration successfully.

With each show, however, the porpoise became increasingly disturbed and frustrated at being "wrong" and the trainer found it necessary to break the rules of the training context and periodically give the porpoise "unearned fish" in order to preserve his or her relationship with the porpoise. If the porpoise became too frustrated with the trainer it would refuse to cooperate at all with him or her, which would create a severe setback to the research as well as to the shows.

Finally, in between the fourteenth and fifteenth session, the porpoise would seem to become almost wild with excitement, as if it had suddenly discovered a gold mine. And when it was let into the exhibition tank for the fifteenth show it put on an elaborate performance including many completely original behaviors. One animal even exhibited eight behaviors which had never before been observed in its species.

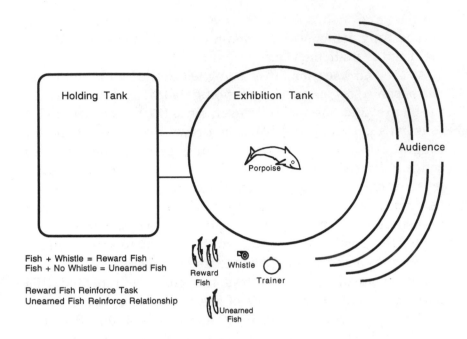

Basic Elements involved in Porpoise Training

The important elements of the story are:

1) The porpoise had to learn a class of behavior as opposed to a particular behavior.

2) The specifics of the behavior was determined by the porpoise, not the trainer. Rather, the main task of the trainer was to manage the context in such a way as to draw new behavior out of the porpoise.

3) The learning problem was context specific (the exhibition tank).

4) The whistle was not a specific stimulus to trigger a specific response but rather a message to the porpoise about something it had already done.

5) The fish given to the porpoise was less a reinforcement for the particular behavior the porpoise had performed than it was a message about its relationship with the trainer. The fish is a *meta message*.

6) Had the trainer not been sensitive to the relationship and taken actions to preserve it, the experiment would have been a failure.

7) Unlike Pavlov, Skinner or a computer programmer, both the porpoise **and** the trainer were being observed by an audience. In fact, it was the ability to please the audience which defined the purpose of the whole training context.

According to Bateson, the stimuli used in such learning experiments are not so much triggers for reflexes, but are context markers that give the animal a clue as to how to interpret the context – a kind of meta message. The whistle-fish combination makes up a context marker that says, "Repeat the behavior you just did." The exhibition tank is a context marker which surrounds the whistle-fish context that says, "Do something different than you did for the previous shows." The relationship with the trainer, as Bateson points out, is the context of the context of the context. That is, the relationship with the trainer is a context which surrounds both of the other contexts. The relationship with the trainer spans the holding tank, exhibition tank, the whistle and the fish. And the context defined by the trainer's implicit responsibility to the audience influences his relationship to the porpoise.

Levels of Learning

Bateson makes the point that, in such a complexity of contexts, there are at least two types or levels of learning involved: Learning I (stimulus-response type conditioning) and Learning II (learning to recognize the larger context in which the stimulus is occurring so its meaning may be correctly interpreted). The most basic example of learning II phenomena is set learning, or when an animal becomes "test-wise" – that is, laboratory animals will get faster and faster at learning new tasks that fall into the same **class** of activity (or make a learning leap like the porpoise in the parable). This has to do with learning classes of behavior.

An animal trained in avoidance conditioning will be able to learn different types of avoidance behavior more and more rapidly.   It will, however, be slower at learning some 'respondently' conditioned behavior (e.g., salivating at the sound of a bell) than some animal that has been conditioned in that class of behavior earlier. That is, it will learn quickly how to identify and stay away from objects that might have an electric shock associated with them but will be slower at learning to salivate when a bell rings. On the other hand, an animal trained in Pavlovian type conditioning will rapidly learn to salivate to new sounds and colors, etc., but will be slower to learn to avoid electrified objects.

Clearly this ability to learn patterns or rules of a class of conditioning procedures involves more than simple stimulus-response-reinforcement sequences for isolated behaviors.

Although Learning II involves reinforcement it is obviously a different logical type than reinforcements for task learning. The reinforcement for "exploration" (a means of learning to learn) in rats is of a different nature than that for the "testing" of a particular object (the learning content of exploration). As Bateson Points out:

"...you can reinforce a rat (positively or negatively) when he investigates a particular strange object, and he will appropriately learn to approach it or avoid it. But the very purpose of exploration is to get information about which objects should be approached or avoided. The discovery that a given object is dangerous is therefore a success in the business of getting information. The success will not discourage the rat from future exploration of other strange objects."
(Ecology of Mind p. 282)

The ability to explore, to learn a discrimination task or to be creative is a higher level of learning than the specific behaviors that make up these abilities - and the dynamics and rules of change are different on this higher level. The importance of the "unearned fish" in the porpoise example - used to acknowledge and preserve the relationship between the trainer and the animal at this higher level - is brought out in the seeming failure of dolphins to perform well at what is called "reversal learning".

In reversal learning an animal is trained to discriminate between two stimuli - say, to approach something when it is shown the color green and to avoid it when it is shown the color red. After the animal has learned to make the discrimination with better than 80% success the 'rules' are reversed - so that it must avoid the green and approach the red. Once again, after it has made the switch with greater than 80% accuracy, the rules are reversed again, and so forth. The idea is to see if the animal will make the switch faster and faster. That is, that it learns on a higher level, "Ah, the rules have been switched again," and makes the transition more quickly.

Most laboratory animals are able to learn the higher level pattern to some degree and progressively become faster at making the switch. Cockroaches, in fact, are apparently quite good at it. The dolphins that were tested, however, refused to continue participating in the experiment after a while. Bateson, who was not involved in the research, talked to one of the trainers involved in testing the dolphins. She reported that since the test was being done as psychological 'research', no unearned fish were allowed because it would be contrary to the strict conditioning procedure required for research. According to her, the dolphins eventually became 'bored' with the whole process and frustrated with the trainers, until they finally refused to 'play the game'. She mentioned that right before the dolphins quit they made an unusual noise. Bateson asked if she had recorded it. She said yes, but because the study was considered a failure, the recordings had been thrown away. Bateson lamented the fact since, according to him, they had destroyed the only existing recording of the dolphin idiom for "*F___ You!*"

Another insightful example of the processes involved in Learning II is Pavlov's report of the development of "experimental neuroses" in his dogs. This occurred when a dog, trained to discriminate between two stimuli, an ellipse and a circle for example, was forced to continue making the discrimination as the stimuli were slowly made to match each other more and more closely (the circle was made flatter and the ellipse was fattened) until discrimination become impossible. At this point the animals began to exhibit symptoms as extreme as refusal to enter the experimental room, refusal to eat, attacking the trainer, and even becoming comatose. Furthermore, not only did the animals' ability to make the discrimination of the circle and ellipse break down but all of the other 'reflexes' that had been previously established to other stimuli disappeared for several months before returning. Pavlov explained the reaction as being due to a clashing together of excitatory and inhibitory responses within the dog's nervous system since one of the stimuli was conditioned to trigger salivation while the other triggered a suppression of that reaction. Yet, this explanation does not account for the severity nor the diversity of the symptoms - which Pavlov wrote off to "character" differences in the dogs.

Why did this conflict of excitatory and inhibitory responses manifest itself in the dogs' refusal to enter the laboratory? Why did they attack their trainers? Why did all of their other conditioned reflexes disappear - and then return?

It seems to me that Pavlov neglected to look at the context and relationships within which the whole experiment was taking place. Naive dogs that had not been pretrained, for instance, when presented with the undiscriminable stimuli did not show any of the "neurotic" symptoms but simply guessed randomly. The fact that the pretrained animals had learned that "this is a context where some definite discrimination should take place", is a necessary preparation for the development of the behavioral disturbance. The circle and ellipse were context markers that said, "discriminate between the two stimuli." The laboratory was a context surrounding that which said, "you must find the one right answer." The relationship with the trainers was the context surrounding both of the other contexts. Unlike the porpoise in the exhibition tank, Pavlov's dogs were given no "unearned fish." When the frustration experienced by the dogs damaged the relationship with the trainers, all of the other conditioned reflexes disappeared because the whole purpose of the training was a function of the dogs' relationship with the trainers. This kind of carryover is undoubtedly what Freud referred to as "transference".

Context and Presuppositions

This notion of contexts embedded inside of other contexts has profound implications for leadership and management; since it is context which determines meaning. For example, Bateson comments that outside of the laboratory situation of isolatable behaviors, stimulus-response-reinforcement exchanges will overlap and "slide" in the sense that different individuals will pick out different stimuli as being the cause or reinforcement of a particular response depending upon the surrounding context. Any particular behavior may constitute a stimulus, response and reinforcement at the same time. The way that an individual perceives or punctuates a particular behavioral exchange, and the way that the individual perceives his or her universe, is a result of Learning II – the perception and interpretation of context. As in the case of the exploring rat or neurotic dogs, the behavioral content and response is punctuated in terms of a larger framework.

Because the reinforcement of higher levels of learning does not come from a specific incidence of feedback or from a particular behavior, it is more difficult to change such patterns. In fact, because behavior can be re-punctuated, Learning II patterns tend to be self-validating. Bateson points out that people in cultures that engage in rituals to make it rain or control the weather won't be persuaded by the ineffectualness of these rituals. If they don't work, they will be inclined to think that the rituals were wrongly performed rather than accept the idea that rituals are futile.

We discover this in attempts to change our accepted psychological paradigms as well. For example, a study was once conducted in which a student wanted to test the ability of animals to run mazes. The student wanted to see if an animal that survived by running natural mazes would learn artificial mazes faster. So, the student decided to condition

ferrets (a long weasel-like animal that feeds on rabbits) since
they had to constantly learn to find food in the maze-like
structures of rabbit's holes.   The student discovered that
when he first let a ferret into the maze, not surprisingly, it
initially went down every blind alley until it found the one
that contained the piece of meat that was the 'reinforcement'.
The second time through the maze the ferret again systematically went down every blind alley - except the one that it
had found the meat in before! Since meat can leave a smell
that lingers, the ferret figured that it had already gotten
what was down that alley and wasn't going to waste its time.
Because of its familiarity with the context, rather than
motivate the ferret to enter that alley of the maze, the smell
reminded the ferret that he had already been down it before.
No matter how many times he tried, the student couldn't get
the ferret to go down the 'right' alley twice. Of course, the
experiment was considered a failure and was never pub-
lished.

Bateson points out that any particular conditioning procedure is both a product and a reinforcement of the larger
system of values or epistemology that spawned them at a
higher level of context. Furthermore, since it is easier for an
individual to perceive the results of his or her behavior than
to perceive the process by which that behavior has been
installed and ordered, Learning II patterns tend to take
place outside of the conscious attention of the individual.

For example, respondent conditioning was developed in
Russia whereas operant conditioning was developed in the
United States. Respondent conditioning tends to breed (and
most likely derive from) a 'fatalistic' model of the world that
says *"You can't control your environment. You have to learn to
respond to an environment that is completely controlled by
someone else. You have no impact on the world but you can
prepare yourself for what is going to happen by recognizing
certain cues."*

Without question, this was the kind of world in which Pavlov's dogs lived. Pavlov meticulously controlled every aspect of their environment; including the amount of light, sound, even the vibrations in the experimental setting. They were put in harnesses so they couldn't make extraneous movements. The timing of their food and every aspect of their care was precisely determined and recorded by Pavlov. They had absolutely no choices regarding their own behavior or activities. It is not surprising that this paradigm flourished in Stalin's Russia. Pavlov was a classic 'Big Brother' figure to his dogs. His epistemology of behavior fit in perfectly with the needs of the context he was operating in.

B. F. Skinner's operantly conditioned pigeons and rats, however, lived in a more capitalistic and entrepreneurial world. The model of the world bred by operant conditioning is, *"You have to do something to survive. Your actions determine what happens in your environment. The signals around you are cues to take actions which, if you do them right, will get you more of something you need or want - but it is up to you to take the initiative and figure out how to do it right."*

No doubt this kind of paradigm was congruent with the epistemology of Skinner's industrial and political America.

Bateson contends that the research involved with these models is less for the purpose of finding the truth than verifying the epistemology of the context from which they come. In the porpoise analogy, the behavior of the porpoise trainer is shaped by his or her relationship with the audience who has paid to come to the show.

Culture and 'Learning II'

Tom Malloy, an NLP researcher and friend of mine, went to Russia in the late 1980's to participate in a peace march with a group of about two hundred Americans. His experience there tends to confirm the higher level influences such as 'culture' and the differences between Americans and Russians. He said that the American group was constantly attempting to participate in the planning of the process: they changed their marching routes if they thought a different way was more suitable; they spent longer amounts of time in some places; they gathered where it was more convenient, etc. This drove the Soviet officials who were overseeing the whole process crazy, because the group was not doing what they were supposed to be doing and following the plan.

Of course, the Americans were not trying to be belligerent or contrary. They were well aware of the political situation involved and, in their eyes, were bending over backwards to be cooperative and not create any problems on an ideological level. They didn't even consider the things that they were doing, which irritated the Soviet officials, to be out of the ordinary. The things they were doing were such an unconscious part of their behavior that they presupposed everyone did it that way.

When the Americans found out they were making the Soviet officials upset they tried to do things to correct the situation, which only made matters worse. Interestingly enough, contrary to the 'Big Brother'/Stalin type of reaction, the Soviet officials seemed more or less unprepared and unequipped to deal with the American's operant style of behavior. After making some initial threatening types of responses, if the Americans did not respond, the Soviet officials didn't know what to do. It was as if the Pavlovian Respondent approach had been so successful that modern

Soviet officials were no longer prepared to deal with people who did not share or respond to the same contextual and cultural presuppositions. Intimate culture contact with the West had been so successfully avoided, that the primary problem was not that of conscious ideological conflict but of unconscious presuppositions about context.

Incidentally, another type of context is required if, instead of producing 'capitalist' or 'fatalistic' laboratory animals, one is to make 'fascist' or Nazi animals. Bateson points out that rats, for instance, are fairly social animals and will not do serious battle with each other very often. However, if you engineer the structure of their training cage (their context) such that there is a scarcity of food and construct a funnel leading to the food that is only big enough for one rat to get through at a time, rats will have to fight with each other over who is to get the food. Bateson reports that if you structure the situation such that a particular rat is always in competition with smaller rats that it can fairly easily defeat, it begins to build a generalization about itself in relation to its environment and fellow rats; that this is a context in which it should be dominant.

A much larger rat is then put in the cage that severely beats the medium sized rat who has always previously been victorious. According to Bateson, the medium sized rat will thereafter instantly and viciously attack anything that is put in the cage, as soon it is placed in the cage - not only other rats, but even objects such as pieces of wood or plastic.

Once again, this is not a case of simple stimulus, response and reinforcement but involves context, relationship to others and generalization that is occurring on another level of learning.

Inside of this paradigm, leadership may be seen more as the ability to create and manage a set of contexts and relationships in which his collaborators can excel as opposed to the ability to persuade others to do his bidding or convince them to follow him.

Implications of the Parable of the Porpoise for Leadership

In the analogy of Bateson's porpoise parable, the 'leader' is the porpoise trainer, the collaborator is the porpoise, the performance tank is the office and the organization or social system is represented by the audience observing the trainer and the porpoise.

The mission of the trainer is not to 'condition' specific behaviors, but rather to get the porpoise to be creative inside of its own natural set of behaviors. The success of the trainer is based on his or her ability to 'draw out' or release the creativity of the porpoise. This involves teaching the porpoise to learn how to generate new behaviors on its own within the boundaries and conditions of a specific context defined by a certain time and space.

The trainer is not some unaccounted for, disembodied, objective observer (as most animal researchers like to perceive themselves) but rather is in an intense relationship with the porpoise. And the trainer's success depends on maintaining the quality of that relationship.

Note that the trainer is being required to use a leadership style that is exclusively based on 'contingent reward' (a transactional style) but is attempting to get the porpoise to learn a transformational task. The "unearned fish" is an admixture of a bit of 'individualized consideration' as part of the trainer's style. The 'contingent reward' of the fish in return for a particular performance is an effective way to get the porpoise to learn a particular behavior. But to learn to generate new behaviors for each performance, the porpoise must 'jump up' to the level of capability. Since the communication limitations between the trainer and the porpoise prevent the trainer from effectively applying 'management by objective', 'intellectual stimulation' or 'inspiration', individualized consideration becomes the only other viable leadership style available.

The relational dimension of the communication is not conducted through 'stimuli' and objectified 'reinforcements' but rather through messages and meta messages about:

1) the state and status of the beings involved in the relationship,

2) the set of contexts in which both the task and the relationship are occurring and

3) the level of messages being sent.

The medium in which the message is being sent is a higher level message about the message being sent.

In order to be successful in releasing new behaviors in the porpoise, both the trainer and the porpoise have to become involved in a higher level learning process. This is a level of learning that has more to do with culture, context and epistemology than with specific behaviors.

As our world and our organizations continue to become increasingly more global and complex, the need to shift our attention and skills to address relationship, culture, context and higher levels of learning becomes even more essential.

Bateson's parable of the porpoise offers an important reference for a new, more appropriate and ecological paradigm for learning and leadership with which to approach the changes of the coming decades.

Applying the Parable of the Porpoise

Leadership is more of a process that is 'revealed' through self motivated activities than taught through techniques. I grow as a leader by feeling a strong will to modify the environment to make it better, then create challenging situations that I can't get out of except by changing. - Gilles Pajou

The parable of the porpoise emphasizes some important principles for leadership and organizational learning, including:

1. The relevance of both task and relationship in learning and leadership.

2. The relevance and difficulties of 'learning to learn' as a part of effective performance.

3. The influence of others (the 'audience') on the activities and relationship between the trainer and learner (or leader and collaborator).

4. The relevance of different kinds of feedback (the whistle and the fish) with respect to learning and leadership.

5. The fact that effective feedback is related to both information (whistle) and motivation (fish).

6. Higher level learning involves self-motivated activity on the part of the learner.

7. Lack of positive feedback can damage the learner-trainer (or leader-collaborator) relationship and cause learners (or collaborators) to 'give up'.

A person attempting to learn to be a more effective leader is a bit like the porpoise in the training tank. He or she must make self-initiated changes in behavior, depending upon the nature of the context, and respond to multiple types of feedback.

In my leadership programs and other training seminars, I often implement a process of feedback based on the Parable of the Porpoise. Individuals engage in activities, involving interactions with others, which are related to defining and implementing their visions. At various points in these activities, people are provided with two types of feedback: "whistles" and "fish". "Whistles" are given in the form of observations about particular behaviors. "Fish" are provided in the form of personal comments reflecting something that the observer liked about that behavior. This type of feedback is not only provided by 'official' trainers and coaches, but by all of the members of the group or learning team. On one level, the purpose of this type of feedback is to identify what someone is doing well and encourage him or her to do more of it. On a deeper level, the purpose is to encourage people to be more proactive, continually searching for ways to improve and become more flexible.

To be effective in giving this type of feedback, people must first learn how to distinguish observations from interpretations. The "whistle" must be based on concrete observable behaviors. The "fish" reflects interpretations related to that behavior. The rule in this form of feedback is that if you make an observation, you must also provide a "fish" (a comment on what you liked about what you observed). Observations without any accompanying interpretations or responses are just data. They contain no motivation or meaning. It would be like the porpoise trainer blowing the whistle but never offering any fish to the porpoise. Feedback provides information when it contains specific data relevant to the task to be performed (like the porpoise trainer's whistle). Feedback provides motivation when the information or the task are made more 'meaningful' (as when the porpoise trainer connects the task to the giving of the fish).

Similarly, if you make a comment about something you liked, you must also provide a description of the specific behavior to which your response relates. If a person is given praise or some other reward but no information about what he or she has done to elicit such a reaction, the person will ask, "What did I do? What is this for?" This is because the individual has no idea what to repeat or how to improve.

For example, let's say a person has made a presentation about his or her vision and mission. When that person has finished the interaction, a group member might say, "I observed that you continually made eye contact with the members of the group (whistle), and that made it easier to feel that we were all part of the same team (fish)."

Thus, the basic form of feedback always contains two key elements:

What I observed:_____

What I liked about it: _____

People are also invited to give "gifts" or "unearned fish" in the form of encouragement or positive comments that are not task related. For instance, a person may say to another, "I appreciate your commitment to congruence and integrity." Or, "Thank you for your support and encouragement." This type of message is primarily focused upon the individual and the relationship. Its purpose is to bolster the sense of rapport between group members.

Notice that this process does not include any negative or 'corrective' feedback. The focus is on what a person is doing that is working well. Just as in our example of the porpoise, the porpoise trainer never threw any 'rotten fish' to the porpoise if he or she did not like what the porpoise was doing. Nor did the trainer impose any other form of punishment or negative conditioning. Rather than giving negative feedback, the porpoise simply received an absence of whistle or fish unless it did something new.

Sometimes people think that this type of feedback eventually becomes ineffective because people build the illusion that they are always successful and are not making any mistakes. And this might be true if it were not for the other elements of the process. As Gilles Pajou points out, in order to "grow as a leader" a person must feel "a strong will to modify the environment to make it better, then create challenging situations that (he or she) can't get out of except by changing." This is where the learner participates in creating the challenge that will lead to his or her growth. The 'illusion' of success is avoided because the learner is encouraged to create "challenging situations" for him or herself. Because the environment is not hostile, the learner is able to monitor his or her own self managed learning path.

In contrast with the Pavlovian and Skinnerian conditioning, the presuppositions of this method of feedback are, *"You are in a context in which it is safe to learn. You can be curious and creative, and challenge yourself. The amount that you are able to learn and grow depends upon your own initiative. It's okay to try new things and make mistakes. Nothing bad will happen to you if you don't perform perfectly at first. You will be guided by concrete and supportive feedback. What is most important is that you do your personal best. You won't be criticized if you don't do it the 'right way'; because there is no one correct way to behave. Rather, the effectiveness of your actions shifts depending upon the context and the type of 'audience' – which you can determine by becoming more aware of certain cues. Thus, it is important to continually explore new behaviors and develop your own awareness, flexibility and self-mastery."*

Keep in mind that the purpose of this type of feedback is to encourage the development of flexibility and the ability to produce new behaviors as an adaptation to a changing context. If a person needed to follow a particular procedure in a stable or threatening context, a process that involved supervision and corrective feedback may be more appropriate. The issue is whether the focus of learning is on the behavioral level or at the level of learning II. The objective of this method of learning is to draw out, 'reveal' and maximize natural leadership ability through a process of encouragement and effective feedback.

The basic steps involved in this method of learning include:

1. The 'leader' is to select a challenging context or identify a challenging 'audience' and present his or her vision and/or path.

2. The leader determines a communication strategy composed of the intended (a) message, (b) meta messages and (c) mix of leadership styles he or she intends to use to communicate his or her vision and path.

3. When the leader is through with the presentation, each member of the group is to give the leader feedback in the following form.

What I observed:_____

What I liked about it: _____

The feedback may be given either orally or in a written form. In our programs we supply "whistles" and "fish" in the form of paper with a symbolic picture on one side and space to write feedback on the other. (In one ten-day program involving 18 people, over 3,000 "fish" were given.) Providing written "whistles and fish" allows people to take their feedback home with them and reread it later on. Some people still cherish and learn from their "fish" and "whistles" years after the program is over.

It is also possible to implement this method of feedback in an organizational environment, either by using verbal or written "whistles" and "fish", or by introducing other methods of providing both types of feedback.

Chapter 9

Conclusion

The purpose of this book has been to present a variety of tools and skills that are vital to visionary leadership. In it we have traced the path from vision to action and have explored some of the abilities required for effective meta, macro and micro leadership. These abilities involve a set of skills relating to the basic 'problem space' of leadership – an *individual* influencing *others* in order to achieve a *goal* within a particular *system*. We have covered skills relating to each element of this 'problem space':

Self Skills:
- Establishing a vision and the supporting levels of processes necessary for translating that vision into actions.
- Creating and maintaining effective internal states by aligning oneself with one's vision and mission.
- Assessing and strengthening the beliefs needed to achieve one's mission and pursue one's vision.
- Developing more awareness and flexibility with respect to one's communication ability and leadership style.

Relational Skills:
- Recognizing and utilizing different thinking styles.
- Identifying key beliefs related to change.
- Exploring ways to transform resistance to change and to strengthen confidence in the future.
- Understanding the relationship between messages and non-verbal meta messages.

- Insuring that the 'intended' and 'received' messages are congruent.
- Exploring the influence of various leadership styles on different people, situations and levels of change.
- Giving effective feedback.

Strategic Thinking Skills:
- Defining a present state and desired state with respect to one's vision and mission.
- Determining a path to the desired state, and chunking that path into manageable steps through the processes of 'storyboarding' and making successive approximations.

Systemic Thinking Skills:
- Considering multiple levels of change and acknowledging different perspectives.
- Understanding the influence of context, mental maps, assumptions and culture.
- Recognizing the impact of different levels of learning and how behavior reflects deeper values and presuppositions.

Taking the time to master these skills will help you to:
1) Feel more motivated and engaged in your work and life.
2) Communicate more effectively with others.
3) Deal more comfortably and successfully with different situations and diverse types of people.

As with many other things, the measure of effective leadership ability is in the results it generates. "The proof of the pudding is in the eating." As Gilles Pajou pointed out, *"Leaders communicate with other leaders through their accomplishments."* Leaders do not communicate through bragging, or threatening or criticizing, but rather through what they are able to achieve through their skill and their vision. It is my hope that the tools and skills in this book will enable you to accomplish more of your life's work and contribute to "creating a world to which people want to belong."

Afterword

I hope you have enjoyed this exploration into *Creating a World to Which People Want to Belong*. As I indicated during the course of the book, other tools and resources exist to further develop and apply the models, strategies and skills described within these pages.

Systemic Solutions International is a training and consulting company established in order to help businesses and organizations define and achieve desired states through the use of NLP based tools and methods. Its mission is to provide the materials and the support necessary to promote effective and ecological change in social systems. The core of Systemic Solutions International is a set of engineered materials for people in medium to large organizations, developed through research projects and training interventions conducted with companies such as Fiat, IBM, Apple Computer, Lucasfilms and the State Railway in Italy. A key feature of the SSI product line is its approach to systemic change which involves a combination of seminars, self learning paths and assisted learning paths. For more information On Systemic Solutions International see **Appendix B**.

NLP University is an organization committed to bringing the highest quality trainings in basic and advanced NLP skills and to promoting the development of new models and applications of NLP in the areas of health, business and organization, creativity and learning. Each Summer, NLP University holds residential programs at the University of California at Santa Cruz. For more information please contact:

NLP University
P.O. Box 1112
Ben Lomond, California 95005
Phone: (408) 336-3457
Fax: (408) 336-5854

Appendix A: Overcoming Resistance to Persuasion

by

Robert Dilts & Joseph Yeager

The taproot of social interactions is, ultimately, our beliefs and values. We purchase items which we believe will give us desired benefits as advertised. We marry because we believe we will be happy with the particular partner we have found. We select careers that we believe will match our skills and ambitions. We have a variety of beliefs about innumerable aspects of reality.

The problem with beliefs is that they are not necessarily true. There is **no instinct** in homo sapiens about what is and isn't real. We build models of the world based upon our unique experiences of it - both sensory and imaginary. And the fact is we can imagine things that aren't real. Furthermore, we cannot perceive reality directly but can only be aware of what comes in through the filters of our senses - which can be quite limiting. It is a tiresome fact, but the brain has to constantly function in a world of uncertainty. Take, for example, the belief that "the world is flat." This seems like a strange belief to our modern world, but how could you prove that it were actually round to someone who happened to believe in the flat version (if you did not have a photograph)?

When you consider that we have many, many such beliefs, the impact of dealing with these beliefs comes into focus as a major issue with profound implications. A customer who believes that a product or service will not be of value can be misinformed. However, simply "explaining" the error of the client's belief is not always likely to change it. If you have ever encountered a jealous spouse, you know that often the efforts made to convince the spouse of his or her mate's fidelity seems only to add proof in the spouse's mind that, indeed, the accused person is guilty. Clearly there is something complex going on in the jealous person's mind that makes the belief seem unshakable.

A bit of thought makes it evident that there is some sort of process going on inside the person that allows him or her to hold a belief in the face of contrary evidence. It is obviously not simple perversity but some method he uses to think about the issue that makes it impervious to ordinary efforts made towards change.

Fortunately, the behavioral science of *Neuro-Linguistic Programming* (NLP) provides successful techniques for communication that are capable of influencing beliefs by identifying a person's system of values or 'criteria'. Let's examine some specific ways NLP can help us change minds through some simple but persuasive communication methods.

In many practical situations, beliefs are "nested" in a way that is similar to the way an onion is organized - layer within layer within layer. To get to the root of someone's resistance to your efforts at persuasion, it is necessary to peel back the superficial layers of resistance. That is, many minor "reasons" are often given in response to a question such as: "Why don't you want to do what I have in mind?" Often two, three or four reasons are offered in a row for the same question. But persistence in the questioning will eventually expose the belief that underlies all of the preceding "reasons." Unless you reach the "real" reason (the core belief and its criteria) that is at the root of their resistance, you are unlikely to be able to overcome the resistance to your effort.

In general people tend to follow Freud's so called "Pleasure Principle." That is, they want more positive experience and less negative experience in relation to any given issue. They pursue pleasure and avoid pain. But, one person's pleasure is another person's pain. People can share the same values, such as "respect," "growth" or "safety," but have different ways of determining how and when these values are satisfied. People may hold a belief as a result of limited experience, a traumatic learning event, or even from having learned an ineffective method of thinking about how to identify a better situation for themselves. In NLP, the term *'criterial equivalence'* is used for the experiences and rules people employ to determine when a particular value or criterion has been met.

One secret of effective persuasion is to identify and then meet a person's core criteria by matching their criterial equivalence.

Often, however, resistance arises because a person has two or more criteria that may conflict with each other. For example, someone might want to make a lot of money in order to be financially secure but somehow never really succeed at it because of an overriding personal belief that people who make lots of money are "surly, uncaring, slick-talking, beasts that siphon off the savings of senior citizens via unsavory schemes." Clearly, such a pair of conflicting beliefs and criteria could hinder a person from achieving his or her financial objectives. Someone else may want to be socially popular but they believe it means being "plastic" or "phony."

There are at least two ways to manage the process of positively influencing resistances coming from limiting or conflicting criteria:

1. You can elicit and <u>contrast</u> the individual's current criterial equivalences with other examples which provide new alternatives or new awareness of payoffs or problems that have not been previously considered.

2. A second alternative is to elicit and <u>disqualify</u> the person's current criterial equivalence and replace it with something more effective.

Either of these choices can give you the opportunity to provide them with alternative criterial equivalences that offer more flexibility and options with respect to achieving their core values.

At this point we are ready to ask: 1) "How do we elicit their limiting criterial equivalences?" 2) "How do we find the alternatives and package the options for them in a convincing fashion?" 3) "How do we install it in place of the original criterial equivalence?"

One primary method of eliciting and changing limiting or conflicting criterial equivalences with NLP is the process of *'pacing and leading'*. In this process one first "paces" by acknowledging and meeting the various surface level criteria until the deeper criteria that are in conflict eventually surface. The criterial equivalences may then be defined and reexamined through the use of leading questions and statements of a certain type. To successfully pace and lead you should remember to never challenge - always pace first and then lead subtly by asking generic questions such as "What do you hope will get accomplished?" "What problems do you think we'll have?" "What outcome do you really want?" "Are you really sure?" "How do you know that's what you really want?"

Once the criteria and criterial equivalence has been successfully identified the quickest way to get a person to reevaluate them is to contrast the current criterial equivalence with examples of experiences where the person has already made an exception to their own criterial equivalence in another type of situation. This is called a *'counterexample'* in NLP. For instance, you may ask "Has there ever been an exception to that?" "Has there ever been a time when this belief was not completely true?"

The following examples illustrate how limiting beliefs and criteria can be identified and dealt with effectively in day to day situations using the pacing and leading process.

The first example involves a multilevel marketing firm whose routine experience indicated that people would attend the presentation of the company, but in spite of smiles and expressions of good intentions, the potential distributors did not follow through and actually begin to sell. When the potential distributors were invited to take action by attending a private meeting with the program leader, lots of excuses and reasons were encountered. The pattern of failed attempts to persuade them to take action indicated that some sort of inhibiting belief was involved. That belief prevented these people from wanting to use the program as a means to make money – which they all claimed they wanted to earn.

One of the authors was hired as a consultant to help solve the problem using NLP methods. The following is an example of how the author applied the process of pacing and leading to identify and change the conflicting criteria at the source of the problem.

Author: Now that you have seen the product presentation are you impressed?

Potential distributor: Oh yes. The products are really impressive.

Author: Well, let's set up a meeting and get you started in the program tomorrow.

P: Oh, I can't. I have to make dinner for my family. *(Value = responsibility to family)*

A: Gee, I wouldn't want you to shun your responsibility to your family. We'll schedule it later. *(Pacing)*

P: I'm awfully busy for a while. *(Value = responsibility to previous commitments)*

A: Naturally, I don't want you to ignore your other commitments. We can work around that. *(Pacing)*

P: I appreciate that, but I think my family will not like me having all of those products and materiasl around the house. *(Value = avoid disrupting family)*

A: Its important not to inconvenience your family. I'll be happy to store it for you. *(Pacing)*

P: Yes but, as you said, I'd need to sell it to my friends to get started. And I don't think it's nice to sell to friends. They might not like it. And besides, selling isn't my idea of an honest profession. *(Core belief and criteria)*

At this point it is obvious that the objections have to do with the belief that selling is an unsavory activity that could make the person unpopular. A way to change that belief is to change the meaning of selling. Here's how it was done.

A: Oh, I understand perfectly. We wouldn't want you to sell. That isn't necessary at all. But since you are such a friendly person, I imagine that you have frequently told your friends about things that interest or excite you. *(Pacing, then leading to 'other' oriented criteria)*

P: What do you mean?

A: Have you ever gone to a movie and been so excited that you told your friends and they decided to go see it because you found it so meaningful? *(Leading question to find counter-example that challenges limiting criterial equivalence for "selling")*

P: Of course.

A: And have you ever gotten so enthusiastic about a new product, say, a new shade of lipstick, that your friends tried it, too? *(Leading question to find another counter-example that challenges limiting criterial equivalence for "selling")*

P: Oh, yes, I have. It's nice to involve your friends that way.

A: Now you know what I mean when I say there is no selling in this program. If you are truly excited about these products and communicate that excitement, you have informed your friends about something that they might want. Then, they can decide for themselves if they would like to purchase it. It's just like telling them about a movie or a new lipstick. You are helping them learn about things they may want. You could consider it as doing them a favor. It doesn't impose on them at all. *(Utilizing counter-examples by asking a leading question to substitute new criterial equivalence for "selling" - "helping your friends learn about things they may want")*

P: I know what you mean. I hadn't thought of it that way. Perhaps we can meet tomorrow, after all.

The essence of this "change of mind" was accomplished by identifying and changing the belief that selling was not "nice." Instead, the author was able to redefine selling as friendly communication about things that others might want to know about. In other words the potential distributor's conflict was resolved by substituting a new criterial equivalence for 'selling'.

Using this process to uncover layers of beliefs, criteria and criterial equivalences can be advantageous in sales and advertising also. For instance, most sales methods involve a process of identifying a group of people you want to sell to, finding out their needs or values, and then trying to make your product satisfy those specific needs. The degree to which you are successful is the degree to which you can directly satisfy those specific values and their criterial equivalences. By understanding and utilizing layers of hierarchies in value systems, however, you can expand on this approach by eliciting and appealing to deeper values in order to attract those whose surface level needs are not directly met by what you have to offer.

For example, let's say you were selling beer. Traditionally, you would conduct a series of interviews with people to whom you wanted to sell the beer, find out what they wanted in a beer, and emphasize through advertising how your beer met their needs. By appealing to a deeper level value in someone's value system, you can expand your market by finding out what would get a person to buy your beer even if it did not meet their surface level needs or desires for beer. For instance, a customer who usually buys the cheapest beer he can find might override that criterion if he is getting something special for someone he likes. That is, he will override his criterion of "saving money" in order to "show appreciation." Therefore, in addition to the people who usually buy your beer, you can expand your customer base by appealing to deeper level values in those who usually would not purchase it.

Consider the following example of using pacing and then leading through the process of counter-examples to expand a customer's criteria for purchasing beer.

Q: What type of beer do you usually buy?

A: Well, I usually get XYZ beer.

Q: Why XYZ beer?

A: It's the kind of beer I always get. I'm just used to it I guess. *(Value = Familiarity)*

Q: Yes, its important to be familiar with what you're buying isn't it. Have you ever bought any other kind of beer? *(Pacing then leading through counter-example)*

A: Sure. At times.

Q: What made you decide to buy it even though you weren't already used to it? *(Elicit criterion of counter-example)*

A: It was on sale. A big discount from its usual price. *(Value = Save Money)*

Q: Saving money can sure help out sometimes. I'm wondering, have you ever bought a beer that you weren't used to buying that wasn't on sale? *(Pace then lead through counter-example)*

A: Yes. I was paying back some friends for helping me move into my new house. *(Value = Show Appreciation)*

Q: Good friends can be hard to come by. Its good to show them how much you appreciate them. Is there anything that would motivate you to buy a beer that was unfamiliar and wasn't inexpensive even though you didn't need to pay someone back for a favor? *(Pace then lead through counter-example)*

A: Well sure, I've bought more expensive beers when I've been out with the guys at work. I'm no cheapskate. *(Value = Impress Others)*

Q: Yes, I guess there are certain situations where the kind of beer you buy can make a statement about your priorities. I'm really curious to know if there's anything that might get you to buy a more expensive unfamiliar beer if there was no one you owed a favor to or that you wanted to make a statement to? *(Pace then lead through counter-example)*

A: I suppose I might if I really wanted to reward myself for doing something difficult. *(Value = Appreciate Self)*

Assuming that this person is representative of a larger population of potential beer buyers, the interviewer has now uncovered some other values or criteria that may be appealed to in order to sell an unfamiliar and more expensive beer to people that might not normally purchase it.

This process of pacing and leading through the use of counter-examples can really help in the process of effective persuasion. By getting people to answer these types of questions you can help them to break out of their habitual ways of thinking and can learn about the ordering of their values.

This information can then be used to get around boundaries that are often taken for granted. One of the authors once taught this method of questioning to a group of men who were shy about meeting women because they didn't think they had anything to offer a woman. They were instructed to go out and interview women and learn to identify values in women that could help them realize that they had more choices socially. The following is an example of one such interview:

Man: What kind of man would you most like to go out with?

Woman: Someone who is rich and handsome, naturally.

M: Have you ever gone out with someone who wasn't particularly rich or handsome?

W: Yes. There was this guy I knew who was really witty. He could make me laugh about practically anything.

M: Are the only people you go out with rich and handsome or witty, or do you ever consider going out with other kinds of people?

W: Well sure. I went out with this person who was so intelligent. He seemed to know something about everything.

M: What would make you consider going out with someone who wasn't rich, handsome or witty, and who didn't particularly impress you with their intelligence?

W: There was this one guy I really liked who didn't have any of those things but he just seemed to know where he was going in life and had the determination to get there.

M: Have you ever gone out with anyone who didn't have money, good looks, wit, intelligence or determination?

W: No. Not that I can remember.

M: Can you think of anything that would motivate you?

W: Well, if they did something or were involved in something that was unique or exciting I'd be interested.

M: Anything else?

W: If they really cared about me and helped me to get in touch with myself as a person..or brought out something special about me.

M: How would you know if someone really cared about you?...

Once again, this dialogue demonstrates how some simple questions may be used to get from surface level beliefs to deeper beliefs and values that can broaden a person's choices and flexibility.

In summary, the process "peels back" layers of resistance through pacing and leading. Then, once the criterion of the most basic resistance is identified, the criterial equivalence may be clarified or expanded through the process of finding counter-examples.

Appendix B: Systemic Solutions International

Systemic Solutions International was established by Robert Dilts (Santa Cruz, California), Charlotte Bretto-Milliner (Santa Cruz, California) and Gino Bonissone (Milan, Italy) in order to help companies and organizations define and achieve desired states through the use of NLP based tools and methods. Its mission is to provide the materials and the support necessary to promote effective and ecological change in social systems.

The core of Systemic Solutions International is a set of engineered materials for people in medium to large organizations, developed through research projects and training interventions conducted with companies such as Fiat, IBM, Apple, Lucasfilms and the State Railway in Italy. These materials cover a number of essential abilities required for people to operate effectively in organizations, including:

- Leadership Skills

- Managing Creativity and Innovation

- Applied Systemic Thinking Skills

- Presentation Skills

- Teaching Skills

- Training Skills

- Self Managed Learning

- Assessment

A key feature of the SSI product line is its approach to systemic change which involves a combination of seminars, self learning paths and assisted learning paths. The engineered materials include learner's manuals, teaching tools and materials, software and other self learning materials. All of the SSI materials are completely modular so that they can be combined and adapted to the individual needs of particular companies and organizations. Certification and licensing arrangements are available for the extended use of engineered materials.

Another level of services provided by SSI involves research and development based upon some of the distinctive competencies of the company's founders in the areas of:

- Consulting
- Tutoring
- Modeling
- Instructional Design
- Trainer's Training
- Certification

As a special service, SSI can also train people within an organization in the skills of modeling, instructional design, tutoring, etc.

In short, Systemic Solutions International provides a coherent epistemology, methodology and technology in support of long term systemic change. This approach offers a number of important benefits, including:

1. A focus on practical results and outcomes.

2. A flexible, modularized system of products and services which may be targeted and adapted to a wide range of specific situations and needs.

3. An emphasis on complete 'paths' of change rather than disconnected seminars and meetings.

4. Multiple levels of services to address different types of organizational needs.

5. Distinctive competence in the area of research and development to help clients stay on the 'cutting edge' and maintain a strong competitive advantage.

6. Use of different types of media and mediums to account for different learning needs and styles.

7. Engineered materials that have been successfully implemented in multinational and national organizations.

For more information about the specific products and services provided by Systemic Solutions International, please contact the address below.

Systemic Solutions International

343 Soquel Ave., #149
Santa Cruz, CA 95062
Tel: (408) 662-6685
Fax: (408) 426-8345

Bibliography

Aubrey, B. & Cohen, P.; *Working Wisdom*; Jossey-Bass, San Francisco, CA, 1995.

Bagley, D., & Reese, E.; *Beyond Selling: How to Maximize Your Personal Influence;* Meta Publications, Capitola, CA, 1987.

Bandler, R. & Grinder J.; *The Structure of Magic, Volumes I & II;* Science and Behavior Books, Palo Alto, CA, 1975, 1976.

Bandler R. & Grinder J.; *Frogs into Princes*; Real People Press, Moab, UT, 1979.

Bandura, A., *Self-Efficacy Mechanism in Human Agency*; American Psychologist, 1982, Vol. 37, No. 2, 122-147.

Bandura, A., *Self-Efficacy: Toward a Unifying Theory of Behavioral Change;* Psychological Review, 1977, 84:191-215.

Bass, B., *Leadership and Performance Beyond Expectations;* The Free Press, New York, NY, 1985.

Bass, Avolio & Goodheim, *Biography and the Assessment of Transformational Leadership at the World-Class Level;* Journal of Management, XIII, 1 March, 1987.

Bateson, G.; *Steps To an Ecology of Mind*; Ballantine Books, New York, NY, 1972.

Bateson, G.; *Mind and Nature*; E. P. Dutton, New York, NY, 1979.

Bennis, W. & Nanus, B; *Leaders: the Strategies for Taking Charge;* Harper and Row, New York, 1985.

Blanchard, K. & Johnson, S.; *The One Minute Manager;* Berkley Books, New York, NY, 1983.

Blanchard, K., Ziagarmi, P. & Ziagarmi, D.; *Leadership and the One Minute Manager;* William Morrow and Company, Inc, New York, NY, 1985.

DeLozier, J. & Grinder, J.; *Turtles All The Way Down;* Grinder, DeLozier & Associates, Santa Cruz, CA 1987.

Dilts, Grinder, Bandler & DeLozier; *Neuro-Linguistic Programming: The Study of the Structure of Subjective Experience, Vol. I;* Meta Publications, Capitola, CA, 1980.

Dilts R.; *Effective Presentation Skills;* Meta Publications, Capitola, CA, 1994.

Dilts R. with Bonissone, G.; *Skills for the Future: Managing Creativity and Innovation;* Meta Publications, Capitola, CA, 1993.

Dilts, R. B., Epstein, T. & Dilts, R. W.; *Tools For Dreamers: Strategies of Creativity and the Structure of Innovation;* Meta Publications, Capitola, Ca., 1991.

Dilts R.; *Changing Belief Systems with NLP;* Meta Publications, Capitola, Ca.,1990.

Dilts, R.; *Applications of NLP;* Meta Publications, Capitola, CA, 1983.

Dilts, R. & Epstein, T.; *Dynamic Learning;* Meta Publications, Capitola, CA, 1995.

Dilts R.; *Strategies of Genius, Volumes I, II & III*; Meta Publications, Capitola, CA, 1994-1995.

Dilts, R. & Zolno, S.; *Skills for the New Paradigm: Lessons from Italy*, ASTD, Spring 1991.

Dilts R.; *NLP and Self-Organization Theory;* Anchor Point, June 1995, Anchor Point Assoc., Salt Lake City, UT.

Dilts R.; *NLP, Self-Organization and Strategies of Change Management;* Anchor Point, July 1995, Anchor Point Associates, Salt Lake City, UT.

Dilts, R., Epstein, T., et al; *Pathways to Leadership* (audio tape series); Dynamic Learning Publications, Ben Lomond, CA, 1991.

Dilts, R. & Epstein, T.; *"NLP in Training Groups";* Dynamic Learning Publications, Ben Lomond, CA, 1989.

Dilts R.; *"NLP in Organizational Development";* OD Network Conference Papers, New York, NY, 1979.

Dilts, R.,*"Let NLP Work for You"*, Real Estate Today, February, 1982, Vol. 15, No. 2.

Early, G.; *Negotiations;* I/S S.M. Olsen, Holbaek, Denmark, 1986.

Eicher, J.; *Making the Message Clear: Communicating for Business;* Grinder, DeLozier & Associates, Santa Cruz, CA, 1987.

Gaster, D.; *NLP - A Practical Technology for Trainers;* Training Officer, London, England, February, 1988.

Gaster, D.; *A Framework For Visionary Leadership,* PACE, Henley-On-Thames, Oxon, England, 1988.

Hersey, P.; ***The Situational Leader***; Warner Books, New York, NY, 1984.

Hersey, P. & Blanchard, K.; ***Management of Organizational Behavior: Utilizing Human Resources***; Prentice Hall, Englewood Cliffs, NJ, 1969.

Kouzes & Posner; ***The Leadership Challenge: How to Get Extraordinary Things Done in Organizations***; Jossey-Bass, San Francisco, CA, 1987.

Laborde, G.; ***Influencing With Integrity: Management Skills for Communication and Negotiation***; Syntony Inc., Palo Alto, CA, 1982.

LeBeau, M.; *Negotiation: Winning More Than Money;* Future Pace, San Rafael, CA, 1987.

Maron, D.; *Neuro-Linguistic Programming: The Answer to Change?;* Training and Development Journal, 1979, 33(10), 68.

McMaster, M. & Grinder, J.; ***Precision: A New Approach to Communication;*** Precision, Los Angeles, CA 1981.

Moine, D.; *"Patterns of Persuasion";* Personal Selling Journal, 1981, 1 (4), 3.

Morgan, G.; ***Images of Organization***; Sage Publications, Inc., Beverly Hills, CA, 1986.

Nanus, B.; *Visionary Leadership*; Jossey-Bass, San Francisco, CA, 1992

Nicholls, J.; *Leadership in Organizations: Meta, Macro and Micro;* European Management Journal, 1 Spring 1988.

O'Connor, J., Seymour, J.; *Introducing Neuro-Linguistic Programming;* Aquarian Press, Cornwall, England, 1990.

Pile, S.; *Vision into Action: Creating a Generative Internal Model of Transformational-Transactional Leadership;* Masters Thesis, Pepperdine University, 1988.

Renesch, J. (Ed.); *New Traditions in Business: Spirit and Leadership in the 21st Century*; Sterling & Stone, Inc., San Francisco, CA, 1992.

Richardson, J. & Margoulis; *The Magic of Rapport;* Harbor, San Francisco, CA, 1981.

Schein, E.; *Organizational Culture and Leadership*; Jossey-Bass, San Francisco, CA, 1988.

Sculley, J.; *Odyssey*; Harper & Row, Publishers, San Francisco, CA, 1987.

Senge, P.; *The Fifth Discipline*; Doubleday, New York, NY, 1990.

Smith, S. & Hallbom, T.; *Augmenting the One Minute Manager;* The NLP Connection, Columbus, OH, 1988.

Tichy, N., & Devanna, M. A.; *The Transformational Leader*; John Wiley & Sons, New York, NY, 1986.

Williams, P.; *New Focus in Differentiating Exceptional Leadership: Identifying and Developing the Potential for Organizational Leadership;* OD Network Conference Papers, New York, NY, 1986.

Williams, P.; *Making Leaders Out of Managers;* Northern California Executive Review; August, 1987.

Wheatley, M.; ***Leadership and the New Science***; Berrett-Koehler Publishers, Inc., San Francisco, CA., 1992.

Yeager, J.; *Collection of Management Articles Related to NLP;* Eastern NLP Inst., Princeton, NJ, 1985.

Zierden, W.E.; *Leading Through the Follower's Point of View;* Organizational Dynamics; Spring 1980.

Zolno, S.; *Scoring a Place in OD: Skills for Transition;* ASTD, Winter 1992.

Index